WADSWORTH PHILOSOPHERS SERIES

ON FOUCAULT

A Critical Introduction

Alison Leigh Brown
Northern Arizona University

Australia • Canada • Denmark • Japan • Mexico • New Zealand • Philippines
Puerto Rico • Singapore • Spain • United Kingdom • United States

Printed in the United States of America
1 2 3 4 5 6 7 03 02 01 00 99

For permission to use material from this text, contact us:
Web: www.thomsonrights.com
Fax: 1-800-730-2215
Phone: 1-800-730-2214

For more information, contact:
Wadsworth/Thomson Learning
10 Davis Drive
Belmont, CA 94002-3098
USA
www.wadsworth.com

ISBN: 0-534-57614-1

Contents

1
Truth, Power, Self

Major Works

Michel Foucault (1926-1984) describes himself as a teacher above all else. For many philosophers, the aim of thinking philosophically has been an increased self-knowledge. For Foucault, the aim has always been transformation. More specifically, he was interested in becoming something other than what he had been given as himself by the various ruses of power. For him that meant exacting from himself a clearer vision of, and making a braver confrontation with, what he elaborates as the chaotic nature of truth.

Because his intense care of self necessitated deep connections with the institutions, persons and ideas which informed him, his work takes on an ethical dimension of trying "to change something in the minds of people" (*Technologies of the Self*, p. 10). He succeeded in producing a body of work that forces its readers to reexamine their relationships to truth, to power, and to self. His ability to teach readers to transform their lives is due, among other things, to his refusal to prescribe a set of universal paradigms for truth, power or self and to his relentless belief that people are free.

In a late interview he summarizes his goals: "All my analyses are against the idea of universal necessities in human existence. They show the arbitrariness of institutions and show which space of freedom we can still enjoy and how many changes can still be made" (*Technologies of the Self*, p. 11). These analyses have the effect of intensifying our experience in the world without a concomitant, and dangerous, desire for power. In his quest to teach his students, his readers, and himself a way of disentangling a contingent order superimposed on things by institutions, he had to rethink the practice of philosophy as such. There can be no more analysis of concepts in isolation from the discourse that uses them in the disciplining of bodies and the creation of institutional forces. Knowledge is not a body of abstract truths nor is it an understanding of some brute reality. Instead, knowledge is an on-going process used as a tool to insert oneself, and one's groups, in a fight against the desire for power.

Desire for power is, for Foucault, a bad thing. In his view, the desire for power is a negative position that attempts to control and stultify rather than to open up and vivify. Using the tool of knowledge must not be allowed to turn into or to stem from the desire to power. This is why, properly speaking, political action must be in the interests only of one's group. To think politically (and hence to act politically) on behalf of other groups, groups with which one is not intimate, is to misjudge any situation at hand. Indeed, it is the desire for power that gives people and institutions the idea that they can speak for and over others. An example comes from Foucault's work with respect to prison reform. His thinking on political action here was merely to listen to prisoners describe their confinement and talk with them about power relations. Prison reform must come from prisoners. This on-going process of knowledge cannot be regulated by the dominant discourses if it is to be in the interest of those described. Dominant discourses are cursed to only repeat the artificially constructed categories of order with potentially devastating results for the bodies under analysis.

Each text is elaborated through the interviews Foucault seems to have graciously and generously granted. The interviews function as a running commentary of the more difficult studies. The Foucault initiate may find that the best place to start reading Foucault is with one of the many excellent collections of interviews and essays. Here, his life and work are shown as examples of how to care for oneself as pleasure in its own right, especially because care for self is the sine qua non of care in the fight against the desire for power. "You see, that's why I really work like a dog and I worked like a dog all my life. I am not interested in the academic status of what I'm doing because my problem is my own transformation" (*Politics Philosophy Culture*, p. 14).

This transformation occurs along an axis of truth, power, and self. Foucault's colleague, the philosopher Gilles Deleuze says of his friend that "these three dimensions—knowledge, power and self—are irreducible yet constantly imply one another. They are the three 'ontologies.' Why does Foucault add that they are historical? Because they do not set universal conditions" (*Foucault*, p. 114). It is important to remember as we begin our introduction to the Foucaultian corpus, that the analysis of these concepts occurs at every level of Foucault's work. He does not privilege one over the other nor does he accord any one of them special ordering status over the other. To be in a position to act with the freedom he posits as the unquestionable fact of existence, we have to come to know these concepts as only ascertainable in specific contexts. In other words, depending on the discourse in which we find ourselves engaged, these concepts will take on different meanings. To be able to make ourselves more ethical persons, persons who are capable of caring for ourselves, we have to study the ways in which truth, power and self operate in the contexts that might serve as arenas for freedom. Whether we consciously accept this challenge toward accountability or not matters little in terms of our actual responsibility. For Foucault, thought and action are inseparable. We are responsible for our actions because freedom is not earned but always already present.

Before turning to the body of this book (Chapters Two through Five) where I will outline the major themes of Foucault's work, a brief introduction to the texts is in order. I have loosely classified the books in five areas: madness and reason, experience and knowledge, delinquency and juridical power, sexuality and self, and the interviews and essays. As Foucault teaches us, any ordering is artificial. This ordering is no exception. The categories, I hope, will be helpful to the reader in choosing where to begin the interesting journey of transformation with Foucault.

Madness and Reason

Four books belong in this category. They are *Madness and Civilization: A History of Insanity in the Age of Reason*, *Mental Illness and Psychology*, *The Birth of the Clinic: An Archaeology of Medical Perception*, and *Death and the Labyrinth: The World of Raymond Roussel*. Each of these books play the concepts of madness and reason against each other and show that when we recognize that insanity and sanity, visibility and invisibility, healthy and illness are constructs of institutions, the experience of our own lives is intensified. The result of this awareness is the possibility of an exteriority, of an outside wherein artful transformation can take place. In *Madness and Civilization*, for example, Foucault argues that a historical analysis of the concept of madness shows that madness itself is nothing. Discourses are attached to certain symptoms and those who exhibit visible and articulable symptoms (which vary hugely from epoch to epoch) are isolated, exhibited, tortured, or cured depending on the time period and the discourse on sanity prevalent at that time. That madness itself is not a thing with autonomous existence is shown through the inability of madness to create, for example, works of art. At the same time, however, without the construct of madness no art can exist. For Foucault art occurs when the painting, novel or composition throws standard interpretations of experience into question. This operation is impossible without a confronting of the nothing that is madness—the place where an individual refuses the order of things given him or her. In *Birth of the Clinic*, Foucault turns his attention to perception itself.

He begins by reminding us that "we are doomed historically to history, to the patient construction of discourses about discourses, and to the task of hearing what has already been said" (*Birth of a Clinic*, p. xvi.) Medical science has adopted over its course, different manners of perceiving the symptoms of diseases that make themselves manifest to the doctor's gaze: "The sign no longer speaks the natural language of disease; it assumes shape and value only within the questions posed by medical investigation. There is nothing, therefore, to prevent it being solicited and almost fabricated by medical investigation. It is no longer that which is spontaneously stated by the disease itself; it is the meeting point of the gestures of research and the sick organism. " (*Birth of the Clinic*, p. 163). As in the first book discussed there is an underlying reality—in this case the body that may live or die. Death is certain to occur. Describing the ways in which doctors came to diagnose the possibilities of life and death, brought the invisible to the level of the visible, the inarticulate to articulation.

In *Death and the Labyrinth*, Foucault takes on the writing of French novelist Raymond Roussel. He happened on to Roussel's work by accident, while in a bookstore ordering something else. Indeed, the chance of his acquiring a Roussel novel on that day was slight. The bookseller was engaged with someone else and Foucault was taking time, something he rarely did, to browse. He later chided himself for not knowing who the author was but quickly devoured the remaining texts and just as quickly wrote the book. What Roussel was doing in fiction resonated with what Foucault was elaborating in the madness and reason books. Foucault writes:

> This is the limit Roussel has deliberately set and traced around

> the marvels of his limitless invention. A rooster can be trained to write by spitting blood, or a rasher of lard can be made to sign in graduated measure (that is the rule of the art; cf. Jean Ferry); skulls reduced to pulp can be made to declaim; the dead can be made to move; but to none of these can the combination of resurrectine and vitalium give back life. The whole order of animal life can be overcome, and mites imprisoned in a tarot card become musicians singing a Scotch chorus, but never does death become life again. (*Death and the Labyrinth*, p. 85)

Intensified experience, art if you will, opens up an outside place for us to try to come to terms with an underlying truth. The truth will be a glimpse of the not-order of things. Death will happen to each thing which possesses life; the discourse on death will reveal to the patient examiner of discourse a historical consciousness of concepts certain to help open up a space for the possibility of transformation. Finding the dizzying place where unreason can be experienced is tantamount to intensifying the possibilities for thought.

Experience and Knowledge

There is hardly a commentary on Foucault's work that does not mention the primacy placed on experience. These commentaries remark on Foucault's unflinching regard for experience at the limit of conventional bodies of knowledge. Experience, for Foucault, is a place to glimpse the outside of discourse and from which to attempt an exit. Institutions will continuously reassert themselves against such attempts. Still, the philosophical position is to press forward from knowledge to experience.

The books falling under this classification (*The Archaeology of Knowledge and the Discourse on Language*, *The Order of Things*, *This is not a Pipe*, and *Maurice Blanchot: The Thought from Outside*) are concerned with what is broadly construed as epistemology, or the theory of knowledge. Deleuze says of *The Archaeology of Knowledge* that it is a "poem of his previous works" (*Foucault*, p. 27). Foucault says that his "aim is to uncover the principles and consequences of an autochthonous transformation that is taking place in the field of historical knowledge" (*The Archaeology of Knowledge*, p. 15).

He argues that a new history must take place; the notion of total history no longer holds with the fabric of our discourses. He will substitute the notion of a general history which will address forgotten histories, reading them into the institutionalized stories in order to explicate them and bring them closer to truth. Problems will arise in doing this new history, many of them methodological. Foucault delineates these problems:

> The new history is confronted by a number of methodological problems, several of which, no doubt, existed long before the emergence of the new history, but which, taken together, characterize it. These include: building up of coherent and homogenous *corpora* of documents... the establishment of a principle of choice... the definition of the level of analysis and of the relevant elements... the specification of a method of analysis... the delimitation of groups and sub-groups that articulate the material... the determination of relations that make it possible to characterize a group.... (*The Archaeology of Knowledge*, pp. 10-11)

These problems for the new history are also the problems for the new philosophy. Foucault struggles with each of these elements in his work. It is no small task to reassemble a body of documents without the old ordering principles. The task becomes reading the documents in a rudderless space in an attempt to tell a new story, this time about how the story came to be told in the manner in which it was told. It is not merely a case of recasting a story from a different point of view. The goal Foucault sets for himself is to recast the conceptual framework itself by making histories of the genesis of the concepts.

Establishing a principle of choice means introducing an element of contingency neither historian nor philosopher finds intuitively comfortable. Foucault is reacting, in part, against Marx and other determinists whose theorizing of the inevitability of world historical events does not seem to be supported by the infinite variation of people's responses to similar contexts. Which details will be included and which methods of analysis will be used are altered by the first two methodological changes outlined. If reactions are contingent, for example, then reductive analyses cannot be used. Most importantly, the inclusion of discourses will be reexamined in light of group's previously ignored. The upshot is a re-reading of the documents of history devoid of the assumptions we have been so well trained to make.

The Order of Things is a wildly ambitious undertaking. Basically Foucault looks at three forms of episteme, or three ways that Western culture, at least, has tried to know the world. He analyses mathematical and physical sciences, the general sciences in which he includes linguistics, living, and economics, and philosophical reflection. Excluded from these ways of knowing are the human sciences that come into existence late on the scene. As the fundamental categories of knowledge changed to include the study of "man," man himself comes into existence. "As the archaeology of our thought easily shows, man is an invention of recent date. And one perhaps nearing its end" (*The Order of Things*, p. 386). Foucault is not suggesting that human beings did not exist but that the conglomerate of so-called universal qualities we associate with human nature arise historically as we begin to oppose nature with human nature in systematic ways. The invention has been detrimental to that which it describes because like all contingent classifications it excludes as much as it proscribes. As it becomes less useful, and we become aware of its harm, "man" will fade away.

In the short works treating experience and knowledge, *This is not a pipe* and "The Thought from Outside"; themes occurring in the major text are elaborated in terms of painting and literature. Foucault pays homage to Magritte and Blanchot, among others, for helping him to see the possibility of an outside total history and dominant epistemological discourses and language. He credits Blanchot, in particular, with helping him to see that language itself has an outside the articulating of which aids in producing knowledge about the coming into existence of man and man's possible disappearance. He writes:

> We are standing on the edge of an abyss that had long been invisible: the being of language only appears for itself with the disappearance of the subject. How can we gain access to this strange relation? Perhaps through a form of thought whose still vague possibility was sketched by Western culture on its margins. A thought that stands outside subjectivity, setting its limits as though from without, articulating its end, making its dispersion shine forth, taking in only its invincible absence; and that at the same time stands at the threshold of all positivity, not in order to grasp its foundation or justification but in order to regain the space of its unfolding, the void serving as its site, the distance in which it is constituted and into which its immediate certainties slip the moment they are glimpsed—a thought that, in relation to the interiority of our philosophical reflection and the positivity of our knowledge constitutes what in a word we might call 'the thought from the outside'. ("The Thought from Outside," p. 15-16)

This thought from outside is the locus of power and is the real space. It is the space of experience. There is no direct access to the outside; still, one can glimpse the outside of, for example, language when creative juxtapositions point in the direction of that possibility. Thus, the reading Foucault gives to Magritte's painting "This is not a pipe" is of interest to epistemologists because the representation of the pipe and the representation of the letters forming "this is not a pipe" push the observer back from the flat representation one can expect from a painting.

Crime and Juridical Power

The two books falling under this heading could not be more different from each other in execution, nor could they be more similar in aim. *Discipline and Punish: The Birth of the Prison* is a treatise on the historical switch from public spectacle of a tortured or killed "criminal" to a disciplined incarceration of the same. *I, Pierre Riviere, having slaughtered my mother, my sister, and my brother...A Case of Parricide in the Nineteenth Century* is a detailed confession written by Riviere in prison with the shortest of introductions written by Foucault. In the earlier books we saw that the mouthpiece for a book taken up into the canon acquires a curious kind of authority. Later Foucault will call such entities author-functions. Pierre Riviere tells his story with its refusals, its fears and brutality with little embellishment or explication from Foucault. Read together with *Discipline and Punish*, the introduction seems to be asking us to think about our relations to juridical power and those over whom it exerts disciplinary control. Foucault reminds us that "on the unique document that is Riviere's memoir, an immediate and complete silence ensued" *(I, Pierre Riviere*, p. ix). This silence is interesting in that the hoop-la surrounding the events leading up to its publication would seem to require some sort of social response to its actions. Instead, the power of panopticism (articulated in *Discipline and Punish*) with its dual discipline of omnipresent observation and unknowable presence shows itself as a cultural response to the delinquency it requires in order to function. That is, the Bentham-created panopticon produced unique disciplinary control in that its structure allowed a guard to be able to see all parts of a prison. At every moment prisoners knew that they could be observed. They need not be observed however because the possibility of being observed was real and easy. People cannot, however, stand the dual uncertainty and omnipresence of observation. They remain silent on the conditions of the many incarcerated members of society. There is no dearth of silence on incarceration in the abstract, especially when coupled with morality. So the noise and silence surrounding the case of Riviere is interesting in what it tells us about the production of meanings through power relations. Foucault writes:

> ...there was Pierre Riviere, with his innumerable and complicated engines of war; his crime, made to be written and talked about and thereby to secure him glory in death, his narrative, prepared in advance and for the purpose of leading on to the crime, his oral explanations to obtain credence for his madness, his text, written to dispel this lie, to explain, and to summon death, a text in whose beauty some were to see a proof of rationality (and hence grounds for condemning him to death) and others a sign of madness (and hence grounds for shutting him up for life). (*I, Pierre Riviere*, p. xi)

One is given in the text documents about the case from doctors, lawyers, judges, and police—all of whom are engaged in the production of meaning, in deciding the life or death of the murderer, and in the various power struggles which had nothing to do with Riviere, his family, or his possibilities. Foucault does not mean to exonerate Riviere nor does he mean to condemn the bodies at work through institutions. His point is that when the voices are placed in juxtaposition to each other, the reader is able to see that there is no reductive explanation for either the crime or its treatment.

Discipline and Punish, in a systematic way, asks the questions: "what stands outside the power of the law?" For Foucault, there are two things: experience and truth. Experience is something like the desire to live freely and well; truth is the desire for knowledge and power that may be channeled toward oppression or toward intensified life. People with similar aims, whether they choose to come together because of previously constructed aims or because they are being disciplined toward a specific aim, find themselves working together. Their efforts are continuously at odds, or even at war, with other groups of people. This network of conflicting and harmonious aims is the fabric of experience. There is no original determination of right grouping, although Foucault seems to affirm that, for example, the obligation to philosophize is more life affirming than the desire to indoctrinate.

Incarceration comes into existence to indoctrinate. The delinquent was necessary to capitalism in many ways. Foucault hypothesizes that prisons exist to transform individuals. Instead of transforming individuals into productive members of society, however, the transformation was to produce a criminal network to protect capital interests and to increase contradictions between members of the working class. The original intent was to make better, more moral, persons and the documents Foucault consults show this. But "the failure of the project was immediate, and was realized virtually from the start. In 1820 it was already understood that the prisons, far from transforming criminals into honest citizens, serve only to manufacture new criminals and to drive existing criminals even deeper into criminality." (*Power/Knowledge*, p. 40).

Showing these contradictions it is methodologically important for Foucault not to assign blame to the various agents. In moments, the anger he feels at the criminalization and psychiatrization of groups at the margins of society comes through in his writing. Still, in order to made evident that these structures are contingent, the contradictions must be explicated in terms of their under-determined fluidity. The texts in this section are ruthlessly political in the sense that their aim is to change consciousness and hence action.

Sexuality and Self

The books here are *HerculineBarbin: Being the Recently Discovered Memoirs of a Nineteenth Century French Hermaphrodite* and volumes One through Three of *The History of Sexuality*. Foucault's position is that in our culture sexuality is at once a secret, a forced confession, and a major determiner of a person's identity. His work in the sexuality volumes exposes various histories of the genesis of sexuality into medical and legal discourses. His brief introduction to Herculine Barbin's memoirs (together with a short erotic novel by Oscar Panizza and a dossier of documents about Barbin) makes clear to the reader his radical position on sexuality.

Barbin is a hermaphrodite. She is born and it is decided that she is a girl. She stays a girl, becomes woman and then falls in love with a woman whom she wishes to marry. Subsequently, she becomes a man. He kills himself. He lives at a time when individual choice with respect to sex determination for hermaphrodites was given up in favor of allowing authorities to make that determination based on expert opinion. Foucault compiles the documents and asks us "Do we truly need a true sex? With a persistence that borders on stubbornness, modern Western societies have answered in the affirmative. They have obstinately brought into play this question of a 'true sex' in an order of things where one might have imagined that all that counted was the reality of the body and the intensity of its pleasures" (*Herculine Barbin*, p. vii). The price of a "true sex" has been heavy in Western culture. The limit case of a person such as Barbin is a dramatic story indicating what has gone awry with the insistence that we name ourselves in terms of our sex and in terms of our sexuality. Foucault's sexual politics flow from the underlying assumptions of his work in this area. He will act as he chooses but he will not identify with a category superimposed by institutions to extract efficiency and meaning at the expense of intense experience and pleasure.

The situation is more complex than a creation of sexual identities and of sex in an effort to control. The true sex becomes that which tells the truth about each of us. "It is at the junction of these two ideas—that we must not deceive ourselves concerning our sex, and that our sex harbors what is most true in ourselves—that psychoanalysis has rooted its cultural vigor. It promises us at the same time our sex, our true sex, and that whole truth about ourselves which secretly keep vigil in it" (*Herculine Barbin*, p. xi). If we understand who we are as a sexed being, we will understand our truth. Foucault argues against this view most forcefully in the first volume of *The History of Sexuality*. A full explanation of this argument occurs in Chapter Five below.

Interviews, essays

I have not addressed the volumes of essays and interviews in these brief overviews. In addition to being good beginnings to the study of Foucault, they stand as Foucault's explanation of his own work, his motives, and his concerns. He comes across in the interviews as a witty, intelligent, deeply caring individual. Throughout the book I depend heavily on Foucault's analysis of his texts. The bibliography lists the major volumes. It is important to remember that Foucault is a critical philosopher by which I mean that he analyses institutions and texts in order to open up new space for thought and action. He does not spell out a program of action, nor would it make sense for him to do so. As he states "my role—and that is much too emphatic a word—is to show people that they are much freer than they feel, that people accept as truth, as evidence, some themes which have been built up at a certain moment during history, and that this so-called evidence can be criticized and destroyed" (*Technologies of the Self*, p. 10).

Influences

As a critical thinker, Foucault's influences are as much those he works against as those with whom he thinks. He was, like many engaged intellectuals in France, dismayed by the events of May 1968 when what seemed like the genesis of a cultural, social, and economic revolution ended before it began. The theoretical backdrop of the uprising was largely psychoanalytically augmented Marxism and phenomenological existentialism. Foucault reacted against these theories not just on their own terms as systems of thought but to the very fact of their, in his view, improper insertion into power relations. His belief in localized transformation, as opposed to total revolution, solidifies at this point.

Marx

The astute reader will have noted that the emphasis on historical context is Marxist in origin. Likewise the assimilation of thought and action is indebted to Marx's views on the material nature of consciousness. Briefly, historical materialism is the view that history is moved by competing interests working themselves out for control of the means of production. Marx argued that in every historical era there is an owning class and a productive class. The owning class wants to keep control of the means of production and the productive class, who produce value, wants to seize that control. The motor of history is that into which a wrench must be thrown. Revolution, thus, must be an economic revolution in the sense that to change the various super-structural forms of oppression, the productive class must take control of and change the economic system. Foucault's difference with Marx is that the priority given to the economic system is probably false in view of the fact that every system is contingent in the ways we have been discussing. For Foucault, the system of prisons and juridical power are in the same power grid as the system of economic distribution. Thus, he is not content to wait for the economic system to change to encourage revolt in prisons. Nor does he imagine that prisons will disappear in the event that wealth becomes equitably distributed.

Marx argued forcefully that consciousness is not the determining factor in historical change, whether that change is ideological, economic, philosophical or scientific. Instead, material reality produces consciousness. For example, Marx argues that Christianity transforms itself in response to economic situations. The move from feudalism to capitalism produces the move from Catholicism to Protestantism. Someone getting an idea and then effecting a change is nonsensical on his view. Foucault is, in a sense, more Marxist than Marx on this point. Marx argues that the owning class controls the dominant ideology. For a revolution to occur, Marx thinks that the productive class must come to consciousness of itself as the producing class. That is, when the class producing the value for society comes to see itself as exploited, that is, as producing value for which they are not recompensed; they will come together as a class to seize the means of production. While there is much debate in Marxist scholarship on this next point, some scholars and activists think that a vanguard class is necessary to effect the change from class to class consciousness. In the more popular writings, Marx certainly seems to argue that a vanguard class is necessary to revolution. The vanguard produces knowledge which it disseminates to the productive class in an effort to speed up it's coming to class-consciousness. Foucault is opposed to vanguard action. Sometimes it seems that his opposition is ethical. More often, however, the opposition is pragmatic. Imposing interests on others does not result in constructive change.

Throughout his career Foucault was accused of being a crypto-Marxist to which charge he mostly laughed. In one interview he wonders "what difference there could ultimately be between being a historian and being a Marxist" (*Power/Knowledge*, p. 53). Always an iconoclast, Foucault fails to cite Marx, in part, because he does not want to appear to be an orthodox *anything* but especially a member of an orthodoxy which he saw as complicit in the sorts of power relations he most despised. Thus, he found it difficult to understand how French Marxists could fail to oppose Soviet incarceration of political and scientific thinkers in mental institutions. Thus he tries to distance himself from Marx in an effort to make clear that he is not what he called "communistological." But the categories of analysis he uses in his historical studies are necessarily those of Marx.

Freud

Foucault's debt to Freud is best expressed in his own words. In

Madness and Civilization, he writes:

> Freud demystified all the other asylum structures: he abolished silence and observation, he eliminated madness' recognition of itself in the mirror of its own spectacle, he silenced the instances of condemnation. But on the other hand he exploited the structure that enveloped the medical personage; he amplified its thaumaturgical virtues, preparing for its omnipotence a quasi-divine status. He focussed upon this single presence—concealed behind the patient and above him, in an absence that is also a total presence—all the powers that had been distributed in the collective existence of the asylum; he transformed this into an absolute Observation, a pure and circumspect Silence, a Judge who punishes and rewards in a judgment that does not even condescend to language; he made it the Mirror in which madness, in an almost motionless movement, clings to and casts off itself" (*Madness and Civilization,* p. 277-278).

We see that even in the critical portion of Foucault's tribute to Freud, admiration shines through. Although Foucault would not like the phrasing, Freud can be said to *humanize* the treatment of the mentally ill, and by recognizing that a cure could never be total, opened up the way for cure to be the aim. Freud actually listened to the patients under his care. He did not go so far as to talk with them. Still, he opened up a possibility for the patient to talk thus informing Foucault's understanding that transformation occurs outside of discourse even though it originates with desires specifically formed around a particular context. Freud helped him to solidify his views that there are no universal concepts which hold for every given case.

Freud's double movement from Observation to observation is important to Foucault's thought about the diagnosis and treatment of the mentally ill. The silent observation of the asylum cannot eventuate in valuable interaction with the patient. That the doctor ought not offer advice or interpretation takes away the moralizing which arises when the patient is an object of study not a subject of transformation.

Nietzsche

Nietzsche is probably the most significant influence on Foucault.

Nietzsche's artful existence and his eventual madness opened up the possibility for thinking the distinction between reason and unreason. Any such opening is crucial for Foucault at every level of his analysis. Classifications, orderings, cover up experience. When a body occurs which successfully resists the orderings, a space is opened for Foucault and others to be sure, to think novelty. Of Nietzsche's lapse into insanity Foucault writes:

> Nietzsche's madness—that is, the dissolution of his thought—is that by which his thought opens out onto the modern world. What made it impossible makes it immediate for us; what took it from Nietzsche offers it to us...*where there is a work of art, there is no madness*; and yet madness is contemporary with the work of art, since it inaugurates the time of its truth. (*Madness and Civilization*, p. 289)

Nietzsche is also the philosopher who for Foucault begins an analysis of power with clearly productive capabilities. "It was Nietzsche who specified the power relation as the general focus, shall we say, of philosophical discourse—whereas for Marx it was the productive relation. Nietzsche is the philosopher of power, a philosopher who managed to think of power without having to confine himself within a political theory in order to do so" (*Power/Knowledge*, p. 53). It is very important to Foucault that Nietzsche does not come from a political perspective. Foucault patterns himself on this model and opens himself up to a great deal of criticism on the way. One could argue, for example, that Foucault's emphasis on power's existing somehow outside discourses (in addition, of course, to its working through power relations) is in itself a political position. In this century, too, not naming a position can lead one to be labeled quietist or apathetic, and ultimately supportive of any fascist tendencies which exist because of silence. (Nietzsche certainly has suffered from this sort of labeling albeit posthumously.) This debate is taken up in detail in Chapter Three.

On a personal note, Nietzsche freed Foucault from academic strictures he thought were hampering his work. On numerous occasions, Foucault mentions that his reading Nietzsche seriously gave him a sort of permission to write as he wished instead of how he thought colleagues expected him to write. He was bowled over by the grace and wit of Nietzsche's writing which writing remained nevertheless philosophically rigorous and meticulously researched. Foucault liked that Nietzsche's research did not translate into a heaviness of text but lays lightly under the surface of elegant prose. Foucault also credits Nietzsche with showing him the possibility of a kind of personal freedom. When he read Nietzsche he would often absent himself from France to work in new places.

It is fair to say that Nietzsche gave him the genealogical method. The genealogical method is a method whereby one traces the hidden or secret history of, in Nietzsche's case, a word to find the shadow contexts of a concept's development. Foucault has commented that his work could be called a genealogy of morals; that is the extent of his obligation to Nietzsche's thought and methods. But he qualifies these comments for two reasons. Foucault thinks that certain things are obvious and that commenting on them draw attention to what is less important about the work. Thus, as we saw in his relationship to Marx, he does not think it is necessary to document a reliance on Marx. Everyone is dependent on Marx. To draw attention to that lineage is to overestimate one's importance. Likewise many philosophers were beginning to look to Nietzsche, and eventually to Spinoza, for alternatives to the imagined rigidity of Marx. To make note of his special relationship to Nietzsche would be to privilege himself above other thinkers who were already seriously working with and through Nietzsche. Foucault sees intellectual thought as thought from the outside. As such, were he to pin personalities to specific work, he would be covering up possible avenues for experience. The second reason is that his genealogy is of far more than morals. In each case, Foucault is interested in exploiting as many connections as possible. His works in the realm of morality but does not stop there.

There is joyousness in Nietzsche that one finds in Foucault. An interesting expression of Nietzsche's affirmation of life can be found in his essay "On the Advantages and Disadvantages of History for Life." Here Nietzsche describes the necessity of doing what could be called minor histories. When one engages in the study of history and notices its implications working themselves out, one could become reactive or cynical. He finds such responses unhelpful and is disdainfully dismissive of persons who acquiesce in this easy position with respect to power. Active and ironic positions assure one a more artful existence. Foucault rises to the challenge.

Minor authors

One assumes that philosophers read broadly outside the field of philosophy. Many philosophers, however, cover their tracks, so to speak. Outside of the field of aesthetics, much twentieth century philosophy refers only to texts that might be properly called canonical within philosophy proper. In contrast to this tradition, Foucault shows his traces and makes the reading of minor texts a part of his method. He is quick to point out that what his critics refer to as minor texts are not in fact minor texts. By so saying, he begins to change the contours of what might be included in the books that eventually make their ways into university classrooms and the history of ideas. The influences he credited throughout his reading are now reissued and made available to readers who might not have heard of them without his careful genealogy of his own thought.

Foucault was reading Roussel while working on the madness books. He credits reading Bataille, Levi-Strauss, Blanchot and Robbe-Grillet for making it possible for him to do his interesting new work. "I was reading Roussel at the time I was working on my book about the history of madness. I was divided between existential psychology and phenomenology, and my research was an attempt to discover the extent these could be defined in historical terms. That's when I first understood that the subject would have to be defined in other terms than Marxism or phenomenology" (*Death and the Labyrinth*, pp. 174-175).

Donald Bouchard expresses how the reliance on minor literatures informs method as well as content in Foucault's work:

> In Foucault, then, we find this constant interpenetration of theory and practice in terms of both his subject matter and method: it begins with the enigma of language which implies a certain theoretical stance, but always in the awareness of its practical implications—Sade's imprisonment, Holderlin's madness; it is elaborated in a larger discursive context with the analyses of Nietzsche, Marx, and Freud and secures a number of allies in Bataille, Beckett, Blanchot, Borges, Artaud, Klossowski, and Deleuze, but always, again, with an emphasis on the practice imposed by this position, whether in the *writing* of literature, in the concern voiced by Freud with respect to the concrete demands of the psychoanalytic session, or in the new theater in which philosophy now finds itself; it gains strength to voice this awareness of so many authors without a name; it deploys this genealogical development and, in doing so, secures its own position and evolves as a clarification of purpose in *The Order of Things* and *The*

Archaeology of Knowledge (*language, counter-memory, practice*, p. 25).

Deleuze

There is a mutual influence between these two philosophers. They refer to each other in their work, they published conversations on important topics, and Deleuze devotes an entire book to the work of Foucault. I think that Foucault gets from Deleuze a political sensibility and a love of life. Felix Guattari's influence must be noted. Guattari wrote many books with Deleuze and brings to the texts an insider's knowledge from psychiatry and radical political activity. Foucault writes an enthusiastic introduction to Deleuze and Guattari's *Anti-Oedipus: Capitalism and Schizophrenia* in which he summarizes the difficult text into rules for living. That they are close politically is obvious from the fact that none of the rules stand in contradiction to rules that can be extracted from Foucault's own works. Another similarity in the thinkers is their refusal to prescribe the rules themselves.

Their joint reliance on Nietzsche is evident from their conversations together and from the introduction to *Anti-Oedipus*. Foucault explains that Anti-Oedipus is any formation of power relations that are in opposition to the restrictions for psychiatry and institutionalization. The adversaries of these joyous formations are the political ascetics or what he calls "sad militants." Additionally, the poor technicians of desires, those who are unable to experience experience (to use Foucaultian language) hinder the creation of anti-oedipal assemblages. The worst adversary, however, is fascism. It is "not only historical fascism...but also the fascism in us all, in our heads and in our everyday behavior, the fascism that causes us to love power, to desire the very thing that dominates and exploits us." The rule which links Foucault most strongly to Deleuze and also to Nietzsche is "do not think that one has to be sad in order to be militant, even though the thing one is fighting is abominable. It is the connection of desire to reality (and not its retreat into the forms of representation) that possesses revolutionary force." (*Anti-Oedipus*, pp. xiii-xiv).

The rejection of the desire for power is present in Foucault's writing. He continues: "It could even be said that Deleuze and Guattari care so little for power that they have tried to neutralize the effects of power linked to their own discourse" (*Anti-Oedipus*, p. xiv). Even a cursory reading of the interviews shows Foucault following this example.

That Deleuze is crucially important to Foucault is evident in this joint tribute to Nietzsche and Deleuze. Nietzsche theorizes something called the eternal return which is a thinking of the possibility that every action, every event, every material connection repeats itself endlessly through infinity. Some commentators believe that Nietzsche offers the eternal return as a thought experiment in morality. Thinking about this possibility forces the question: "Is this the life you wish to revisit?" Others opine that it is Nietzsche's attempt to come to terms with the then-nascent art of astrophysics. Both of these readings see the return as bringing things back into a circle of dialectical thought. Deleuze, for Foucault, breaks spectacularly from an endless re-assimilation of difference into the same. The tribute:

> We must avoid thinking that the return is the form of a content which is difference; rather, from an always nomadic and anarchical difference to the unavoidably excessive and displaced sign of recurrence, a lightning storm was produced which will one day be given the name of Deleuze: new thought is possible; thought is again possible (*language, counter/memory, practice,* p. 196).

Foucault, then, is influenced by many and diverse thinkers, artists, and social-intellectual practices. His work is determined by contemporary political events and eventually becomes determining, in discernible part, of future events. Far from posing a clean break with significant thinkers who come before him, his work is an extension of previous systems of thought. His work offers methodologies for re-conceiving manners of doing epistemology, political theory, moral theory, and ethical theory. The epistemology affects every other aspect of his work and contains the major concept a student of Foucault should know. In the next chapter, we become acquainted with that epistemology.

2
Epistemology

Epistemology is the study of knowledge. For centuries western philosophy has favored epistemologies that worked toward certain, foundational truths whose implications would culminate in Truth. A person could be said to know that a proposition was true if that person were a unified subject able to assert the proposition, knowingly, with no possibility of doubt. The knowing subject was believed to be morally better than those who failed to know truths and did not devote their lives opening up ways to possible Truth. All systems of thought have exceptions; within the canon of western philosophy there are exceptions to this rule. Still, it was not until the twentieth century when exceptions to the belief that subjects could and should know Truth became as widespread as the traditional rule.

One of the last traditional epistemological doctrines to come under attack was that to know a proposition one had first to believe it. The early work of the Cambridge philosophers and simultaneous work being done by phenomenologists opened a way for Foucault to arrive at a position that denies an epistemological place for individual intentions. So, while Foucault's epistemology may seem oddly de-centered with respect to subjective knowledge, he is working out of a fairly standard philosophical position. As they do, he starts with experience.

Experience

As we have seen in our introduction to the Foucaultian corpus, the concepts on which he works are interrelated in complicated and inextricable ways. There is a seemingly unified aim, however, of coming to understand oneself through a relentless juxtaposition of bodies of knowledge with experience. This juxtaposition results, when successful, in an enhanced understanding of the competing discourses busy at constructing fields of power which, if left to their own devices, would define and control us. There is no absolute knowledge nor is there absolute truth. There are more or less informed manners of positioning oneself with respect to the power relations in which one finds oneself. Foucault remarks: "knowledge is for me that which must function as a protection of individual existence and as a comprehension of the exterior world. I think that's it. Knowledge as a means of surviving by understanding" (*Politics, Philosophy, Culture*, p. 7).

A simple schematic of Foucault's epistemology has to include at least three elements: experience, power/knowledge, and discourse. These are the categories to which we will turn our attention. As we move through these connected categories, it is helpful to keep in mind some key points about methodology. Foucault is moving in the direction of the general history we have previously noted. Some commentators divide his work into the archaeological and the genealogical periods. Foucault himself resisted the distinction but it is helpful to think of them separately in order to get a better handle on the manner in which Foucault practices epistemology.

Foucault's description of archaeology follows:

> The horizon of archaeology, therefore, is not a science, a rationality, a mentality, a culture; it is a tangle of interpositivities whose limits and points of intersection cannot be fixed on a single operation. Archaeology is a comparative analysis that is not intended to reduce the diversity of discourses, and to outline the unity that must totalize them, but is intended to divide up their diversity into different figures. (*The Archaeology of Knowledge*, pp. 159-160)

Foucault is engaged in a practice of discovery wherein one must not posit an endpoint in advance. One might argue that no quest for knowledge presupposes its endpoint—if one knows the outcome of a line of thought, one would have already performed the mental operation. Foucault is making a more dramatic claim. He is asking that our researches fail to have even a formal aim. Thus, he wants us to think whatever our object or subject of thought is insofar as possible from the categories that have surrounded it.

A reader might interject—how does this differ from any method of doubt—even one going as far back as Descartes. Students of philosophy will recall that Descartes asks his readers to perform a thought experiment during which they suspend all assumptions. Descartes has as his aim, however, certain knowledge. Foucault does not want so much a suspension of assumptions as a suspension of ordering in a framework where the nature of the outcome is not assumed. His question might be posed as "What would happen if we rethink madness, for example, outside of the systems of classifications of the discourses which exert their power on the 'mentally ill?'."

At the same time that he is practicing archaeology, he seems to always already be engaged in genealogical practices. Following the genealogical method, one reads everything one can find about the subject or object in question trying to trace the shifts in meanings of key, controlling terms. In practical terms, these methods seem inseparable in Foucault's work. The question concerning the suspension of ordering works alongside the questions: "What has been recorded about this concept in the relevant time period that previous thinkers have failed to address? How much of the *absent* discourse informs the practices surrounding the concept?"

Interiority

I have been putting off one of the more difficult concepts in Foucault but to many of his readers, one of the most exciting. Namely, Foucault does not give credence to the view that the individual has an inner life. It is not that he does not think we have access to all of our inner musings and workings, as does for instance Freud. He does not think that there is an inner life. Earlier it came out that Foucault has argued that the concept "man" is a recent invention. Following Nietzsche, he holds the view that the human soul is an older invention, but an invention nonetheless. Everything we know, we know through observation of external relations. When we have been referring to the "outside" it is to something beyond the outside which might properly refer to the conceptual placeholder for external relations. Thus, for example, when Foucault said that for him knowledge must function as a comprehension of the exterior world, exterior does not refer to objects outside of a subject. Instead, he is referring to an outside of the discourse in which one is currently engaged, or, more dramatically, the outside that is glimpsed by colliding discourses.

Deleuze explains the doubling of externalities in his book on Foucault where he writes:

> This is Foucault's major achievement: the conversion of phenomenology into epistemology. For seeing and speaking means knowing [savoir], but we do not see what we speak about, nor do we speak about what we see; and when we see a pipe we shall always say (in one way or another): 'this is not a pipe', as though intentionality denied itself, and collapsed into itself. Everything is knowledge, and this is the first reason why there is no 'savage experience' there is nothing beneath or prior to knowledge. But knowledge is irreducibly double, since it involves speaking and seeing, language and light, which is the reason why there is no intentionality. (*Foucault*, p. 109)

In phenomenology, the bodily apprehension of appearances is the place from which one begins knowing. That is, the building blocks of knowledge are the innumerable pieces of indubitable knowledge that the sensations one has are "true." The experiences one has with the external world need not, and indeed, cannot be doubted. These experiences are foregrounding for every linguistic operation that might result in valid knowledge claims. Another way to put this is that there is a body of experiences that we never notice because they are so obvious. These experiences are the brute, untheorized, raw material of knowing. Foucault does not think that these raw experiences exist. There is always some warring force calling into question the ordering of our perceptions. Thus, as Deleuze says, each seeing is accompanied by a saying and each saying by a seeing which contradict each other external to what has traditionally been called the subject.

Is there a pipe?

Deleuze's example of the pipe that is never a pipe comes from Foucault's reading of Magritte's painting. Perhaps a non-philosopher's attempt to discuss these issues will make them more clear. Magritte engaged in a very brief correspondence with Foucault—three letters were exchanged. In a letter dated May 23, 1966 Magritte praises Foucault's *The Order of Things* and then writes: "Things do not have resemblances, they do or do not have similitudes. Only thought resembles. It resembles by being what it sees, hears, or knows; it becomes what the world offers it. It is as completely invisible as pleasure or pain...For a time a curious priority has been accorded 'the invisible,' owing to a confused literature, whose interest vanishes if we remember that the visible can be hidden, but the invisible hides nothing; it can be known or not known, no more." (*This is not a pipe*, p. 57). If we think of thought becoming what the world offers it, it is hard to think of a thinking thing preexisting articulation, vision, or knowledge. Thought is invisible and as such is known or not known with no gradation.

On June 4, 1966 Magritte writes again. He continues in similar vein: "...nothing is confused save the mind that imagines an imaginary world. I am pleased that you recognize a resemblance between Roussel and whatever is worthwhile in my own thought. What he imagines evokes nothing imaginary, it evokes the reality of the world that experience and reason treat in a confused manner" (*This is not a pipe*, p. 58).

Deleuze tries again to explain the absence of intentionality through a double movement of knowing. Knowing can take hold in knowledge-Being or power-Being. Experience is already a knowing and all knowing is already embedded in contexts of a struggle for power. There is a kind of knowing which is somewhat consonant with itself as a set of relations and knowing which is overtly working toward, or against, such consonance. The first form can appear as interiority but it takes an operation of imagining an imaginary world to then posit that appearance as a reality. The second form, referred to as strategic, appears as and is exteriority. Deleuze writes:

> If knowledge is constituted by two forms, how could a subject display any intentionality towards one object, since each form has its own objects and subjects? Yet it must be able to ascribe a relation to the two forms, which emerges from their 'non-relation'. Knowledge is Being, the first figure of Being, but Being lies between two forms. ...But this double capture, which is constitutive of knowledge-Being, could not be created between two irreducible forms if the interlocking of opponents did not flow from an element that was itself informal, a pure relation between forces that emerges in the irreducible separation of forms. This is the source of the battle

> or the condition for its possible existence. This is the strategic domain of power, as opposed to the stratic domain of knowledge. From epistemology to strategy. This is another reason why there is no 'savage' experience, since battles imply a strategy and any experience is caught up in relations of power. This is the second figure of Being, the 'Possest', power-Being, as opposed to knowledge-Being. It is the informal forces or power-relations that set up relations 'between' the two forms of formed knowledge. The two forms of knowledge-Being are forms of exteriority, since statements are dispersed in the one and visibilities in the other; but power-Being introduces us into a different element, an unformable and unformed Outside which gives rise to forces and their changing combinations. (*Foucault*, pp. 112-13)

So, there is no internal subject; indeed, there is no subject to speak of. The outside is doubled and each of the double exteriorities carries its own contradictions. Each act of knowing becomes strategic precisely because there is no private knowing, properly so-called.

The Witching Double

Foucault's use of Magritte's drawing is constructive not only because it is a good example of his use of experience in knowledge but also because the example includes, in an obvious manner, vision and speech: saying and seeing. There is a drawing behind the drawing that we experience prior to coming into contact with Magritte because what Magritte has captured is the double movement of knowing. Foucault credits Magritte with exposing this double movement:

> I cannot dismiss the notion that the sorcery here lies in an operation rendered invisible by the simplicity of its result, but which alone can explain the vague uneasiness provoked. The operation is a calligram that Magritte has secretly constructed, then carefully unraveled. Each element of the figure, their reciprocal position and their relationship derive from this process, annulled as soon as it has been accomplished. Behind this drawing and these words, before anyone has written anything at all, before the formation of the picture (and within it the drawing of the pipe), before the large, floating pipe has appeared—we must assume, I believe, that a calligram has

> formed, then unraveled. There we have evidence of failure and its ironic remains. (*This is not a pipe*, p. 20)

Magritte thus shows us what is complicated for philosophers to say: that at one and the same time we deny a false reality and affirm the signs thereof:

> Each element of 'this is not a pipe' could hold an apparently negative discourse—because it denies along with resemblance, the assertion of reality resemblance conveys--but one that is basically affirmative: the affirmation of the simulacrum, affirmation of the element within the network of the similar. (*This is not a pipe*, p. 47)

Power

A first response when encountering an epistemology that denies interiority to the knowing subject might be "Who or what is the thing that knows?" Epistemology is the study of knowledge; things that are capable of uttering "I" are the sorts of things we think of as knowing. Indeed, Foucault himself starts with the questions: "What can I do? What do I know? What am I?" These questions are not asked of a unified knowing subject but of a constructed "I." As such they cannot be adequately answered without a more careful analysis of his conception of power to which we now turn.

Power/Knowledge

Processes of Subjectivation

For some philosophers to know one meant knowing the contents of one's mind. Self-knowledge, then, could be achieved by contemplation of self-evident truths. Most of us mean something quite different than this when we think of following the Delphic oracle to "know thyself." Written in the temple, it served as a reminder to know one's place, to know that one was not a god, to understand one's positioning with respect to the powers that be. Socrates takes up the oracle and transforms it into a principle for living wisely, for knowing the extent of one's ignorance. A contemporary reinterpretation mutates it further to include quite contemplation, but to extend itself to a challenge to test one's limits intellectually, physically, and emotionally. We might ask ourselves: "What stuff am I made of?" hoping that it is the right stuff. This is appropriate for Foucault since it captures both the power relations—who I am in a social hierarchy—and contains the irony implicit in a naïve uttering of "self."

Philosophers working in the France during the middle of this century could not help but be heavily influenced by the work of German philosopher G.W.F. Hegel. Foucault is not an exception. He studied with Louis Althusser who was influenced by Hegel if only through Marx. Hegel makes the injunction to know oneself immensely difficult. His *Phenomenology of Spirit* is an exegesis of Spirit coming to know itself as Spirit as it develops its consciousness. The outcome of Spirit's journey through consciousness was Absolute Knowing. The spirit that could recognize itself as spirit would have to know everything that could be known. The story is told that when Hegel recognized what he had discovered, that it is possible to know everything, at least in theory, he went quite mad. For a period of time he could not speak and was thrown into a deep depression. He quickly realized that his discovery was merely formal. The form of all knowing could be outlined. Filling in the details of the particulars would follow, as the form's content that it had to be. As such there was still the possibility of important work even though the movement of history had been fully accounted. A Hegelian might read Foucault as filling in the details of the form that an all-knowing subject already knows. It perhaps goes without saying that Foucault would reject the subject position of Hegel's scribe.

Foucault's manner of answering the questions "What can I do? What do I know? What am I?" is a blend of the philosophical traditions which precede him. After he loses the imperative to both eternal certainty and totalizing discourse, he is able to perform the meaningful activity of self-knowledge by contemplation of concepts, knowing his place in power relations, finding the limits of his possible experience, and knowing everything. For him, however, the contemplation of concepts involves moving targets within power relations wherein he might find his place. For instance, if one were a university student, to know oneself would have to involve understanding the nature of the university system in which one finds oneself. As consumers of mass media some research into the grids of power, which produce and disperse the relevant entertainment is in order. Knowing oneself then is knowing everything about the discourses that form the processes of ones particular coming to be subject. Deleuze describes the difference between coming to know oneself under the rubric of the individual complete with interiority and coming to know oneself the Foucaultian way:

> He does not write a history of private life but of the conditions governing the way in which the relation to oneself constitutes a private life. He does not write a history of subjects but processes of subjectivation, governed by the foldings operating in the ontological as much as the social field. In truth, one thing haunts Foucault—thought. The question: "What does thinking signify? What do we call thinking?' is the arrow first fired by Heidegger and then again by Foucault. He writes a history, but a history of thought as such. To think means to experiment and to problematize. Knowledge, power and the self are the triple root of the problematization of thought. (*Foucault*, p. 116)

Understanding subjects requires understanding the concept "subject" and then coming to terms with what an internal thought process could entail or mean. That problem, a relatively new problem for epistemology, requires contemplating knowledge, power and self.

Examples of Power/Knowledge

We have been abstract long enough. As noted, Foucault offers a running commentary of his work in interviews. Two examples should suffice to show what Foucault is trying to illuminate in his researches into the understanding of discourses. One case where knowledge and power come together to produce a discourse which in turn creates a new set of power relations involves children's sexuality. This case is especially interesting because science "discovered" children's sexuality and in the process "created" it. The second example involves an analysis of bio-power to explain the interplay of power-relations normally called capitalism.

Foucault explains his notion that power is a positive force in the production of knowledge. Often power is thought of an oppressive force which prohibits or represses, but power opens up new relations as well. He says:

> Now if you read all the...manuals for parents that were published in the eighteenth century...you find that children's

> sex is spoken of constantly and in every possible context. One might argue that the purpose of these discourses was precisely to prevent children from having a sexuality. But their *effect* was to din it into parents' heads that their children's sex constituted a fundamental problem...The result was a sexualising of the infantile body, a sexualising of the bodily relationship between parent and child, a sexualising of the familial domain. 'Sexuality' is far more of a positive product of power than power was ever repression of sexuality. (*Power/Knowledge*, p. 120)

The sorts of knowledge claims that we really care about making involve our relations within fields of power. It becomes problematic to make legitimate claims about, for instance, the sexuality of children, if we fail to take account of what it means to say that the same could be "discovered." Furthermore, failing to ask the right kinds of questions surrounding the sorts of claims we might be willing to make allows conceptual mistakes to abound. The problem for Foucault is to discover "why the West has insisted for so long on seeing the power it exercises as juridical and negative rather than as technical and positive" (*Power/Knowledge*, p. 121).

Teasing out answers to this question is helpful in examining something as large scale as the advent of capitalism. Foucault argues that a new form of power arises during the eighteenth century, a power he calls bio-power. This is a power that exerts itself on the organization and disciplining of life. Because of a brisk development in the disciplines which coincided with an ever-increasing and more mobile population, "there was an explosion of numerous and diverse techniques for achieving the subjugation of bodies and the control of populations, marking the beginning of an era of 'bio-power'" (*The History of Sexuality*, p. 140).

Foucault claims that the development of capitalism would not have been possible had it not been for bio-power:

> [the development of capitalism] would not have been possible without the controlled insertion of bodies in the machinery of production and the adjustment of the phenomena of population to economic processes. But this was not all it required; it also needed the growth of both these factors, their reinforcement as well as their availability and docility; it had to have methods of power capable of optimizing forces, aptitudes, and life in

> general without at the same time making them more difficult to govern (*The History of Sexuality*, p. 141).

At every turn the explanations of Foucault's understanding of knowledge turn to morality, ethics, sexuality, politics, and economics. A description of his conception of truth will illuminate why we can't stay confined to truth tables or scientific method.

Truth and Power

For Foucault, truth is never outside of power. There is no truth that is not in the struggle of power relations. It should be noted also that truth does not lack power. Truth's currency has always been in demand. Whatever truth there is, is solidly in this world. It is not something one will discover somewhere else or at some other time. There are only the truths which have currency here and now. Every society has what Foucault calls a regime of truth. These regimes determine which discourses are allowed and which are not. One of the restrictions on truth is who gets to own and produce it. In our society, Foucault argues, it is mostly produced and determined by universities, armies, media and writing.

Different societies will have different sites for the production of truth. Foucault suggests that truth possess at least five traits in what he calls "our society." Scientific discourse is the major center of truth. Economics and politics are always involved in the production and dissemination of truth. Truth circulates through society mostly unhampered. There is an ideological battle over the ownership of truth. Finally, only a few political and economic apparatuses are allowed to name truth. With this description of truth, epistemology is necessarily political and ethical.

The Omnipresence of Power

That power is everywhere for Foucault has been the subject of the most heated criticism against him. Theorists don't usually like a concept to be applicable across the board because the significance of the concept tends to drop out. The thesis that power is everywhere becomes most important in our discussion of politics in Chapter Three. For now it is imperative to note that Foucault believes that there is no outside to power. Everyone has power and everyone has power exerted against or for him or her. This does not mean that one is forever dominated or boxed in. It means that every interaction involves participation.

The most popular way that the latter point has been made is that there is no power without resistance. No discourse of truth goes unchallenged. Discourses are arenas for studying power relations. While some epistemologists study the truth-value of propositions and the manners in which to ascertain the validity of our coming to know that we know these propositions, Foucault is concerned with coming to understand discourses. As we have seen knowledge is contested at two levels: experience and power. Discourses are loci of knowledge. Like experience and power, discourses are neither stable nor monolithic. No discourse could cover the diversity of truths.

Discourse

Discourse is not mere language. A discourse is a system of rules regulating the flow of power (both positive and juridical) which serves a function of promoting interests in a battle of power and desires. Once located it is a field for analysis which analysis is a central portion of our coming to know ourselves. As such, a discourse is an aid to understanding. A discourse is not identified except in observing a moment of significant change. In *The Birth of the Clinic* Foucault poses this question for himself: "From what moment, from what semantic or syntactical change, can one recognize that language has turned into a rational discourse?" (*The Birth of the Clinic*, p. xi). These moments are those that reveal the most to our potential understanding. Foucault's aim in pinpointing and then delineating discourse is described like this:

> If I spoke of discourse, it was not to show that the mechanisms or processes of the language (langue) were entirely preserved in it; but rather to reveal, in the density of verbal performances, the diversity of possible levels of analysis; to show that in addition to methods of linguistic structuration (or interpretation), one could draw up a specific description of statements, of their formation, and of the regularities proper to discourse (*The Archaeology of Knowledge*, p. 200).

There is not one dominant discourse. In thinking about discourse it is sometimes helpful to think pictorially. Imagine a series of circles each of which constitutes a discourse. One could name them psychoanalytic discourse, discourse of sexuality, incarceration discourse, prisoner's discourse, university discourse and so on. No discourse stands alone and no discourse is complete. The discourses interrelate and intersect each other in a continuously moving plane. Language exists prior to any given discourse. The pre-discursive language does not exert juridical or disciplinary power. Some of the discourses do not interpenetrate but are quite independent of each other. For Foucault, there is nothing about those relations, which transcends the place of those relations. He writes:

> Discursive relations are not...relations exterior to discourse, relations that might limit it, or impose certain forms upon it, or force it, in certain circumstances to say certain things. They are, in a sense, at the limit of discourse: they offer it objects of which it can speak, or rather...they determine the group of relations that discourse must establish in order to speak of this or that object. (*The Archaeology of Knowledge*, p. 46)

Where is the foundation, then, of these discourses? It seems a fair question to ask of Foucault that since we are asked to give up brute experience and we are asked to think of language as only contingently determining any given discourse, that some foundation for our knowledge must be posited. Surely there must be some stuff, some substance at the base of our discourses of power.

Foucault answers this sort of question by explaining the genesis of such questions. Language is a necessary presence for any discourse to take place; but there is no necessary connection between the discourses. Any given discourse could always be other than it is. Our impulse to look for necessary questions is a result of our buying into the discourse of rationality. If we return for a moment to our example of the relationship between bio-power and capitalism, the abstract treatment of relations is more evident. Bio-power does not exist outside of capitalism any more than capitalism determines the manners in which we control, for example, population. Or, to return to the other example, infant sexuality does not exist outside of discourse. Its being is dependent on the manner in which we write and discourse about it.

In noting the relationships Foucault has with Freud and with Marx it is clear now that the difference is primarily at the level of epistemology. Both Freud and Marx thought of themselves as doing science in fairly traditional ways. They both discover a deeper reality about the actual world. Foucault's difference is that he sees them as creating the objects and subjects of study by producing the most powerful truth discourse available.

Functions of Discourses

We will come to the political uses of discourses in the next chapter. It is important to note that in coming to terms with Foucault's epistemology we must think about the functions of discourse in the production of truth. The reader may be frustrated that the categories of analysis in Foucault are hard to keep separate. Not all philosophers have separated out their ethics from their epistemologies, however. For instance Plato and Spinoza both make the road to knowledge synonymous with the road to being moral or ethical. It is less common in philosophers, especially prior to Marx, to have epistemology so linked with politics. Discourses function to produce truth. Truth is not out there waiting to be discovered, it is created in the interest of those who exert the most power.

> To *discover*, therefore, will no longer be to *read* an essential coherence beneath a state of disorder, but to push a little farther back the foamy line of language, to make it encroach upon that sandy region that is still open to the clarity of perception but is already no longer so to everyday speech—to introduce language into that penumbra where the gaze is bereft of words. (*The Birth of the Clinic*, p. 169)

The connection between politics and truth-production is not simple battling over interests, however. This would not make an interesting epistemology. For Foucault these economical and political interactions produce not just the truths of the conditions of people's lives but the categories of epistemology themselves. So for instance, when "studying" and "controlling" madness the ways in which sight and expression functioned in particular medical discourses radically changed as the mental hospital came to be:

> It was also necessary to open up language to a whole new domain: that of a perpetual and objectively based correlation

> of the visible and the expressible. (*The Birth of the Clinic*, p. 196)

This necessity was not linked to an improved treatment of the mentally ill. The necessity was linked to discourses of rationality and discourses of morality both of which worked through the doctors and through the discourses of all parties' interpenetration. There was not a philosopher sitting somewhere who came up with the theory of positivism; rather, the interplay of discourses surrounding, in this instance, reason and unreason, produce the theory before it is articulated.

> In particular, that with which phenomenology was to oppose it so tenaciously was already present in its underlying structures: the original powers of the perceived and its correlation with language in the original forms of experience, the organization of objectivity on the basis of sign values, the secretly linguistic structure of the datum, the constitutive character of corporal spatiality, the importance of finitude in the relation of man with truth, and in the foundation of this relation, all this was involved in the genesis of positivism. (*The Birth of the Clinic*, p. 196)

The formation of systems of thought take the same doubling as thinking itself. There is the relationship between the self to itself as a thing coming to knowledge through its external relations and the relationship to the network of discourses.

> The mobility of the system of formation appears in two ways. First at the level of the elements that are being related to one another: these in fact may undergo a number of intrinsic mutations that are integrated into discursive practice without the general form of its regularity being altered...But inversely the discursive practices modify the domains that they relate to one another. (*The Archaeology of Knowledge*, pp. 73-5)

The discourses function "internally" and they work on each other at the "second" level.

At root what keeps everything going is a warring element between discourses and groups of subjects. "Contradiction, then, functions throughout discourse, as the principle of its historicity" (*The Archaeology of Knowledge*, p. 151).

Analysis of Discourses

A major aim of Foucaultian analysis is to understand the institutions that have created social, political, cultural, and economic space. His analysis is always a "doing." W.V.O. Quine remarks that a change in logic is a change in the world. Foucault would have to concur with him. Thinking through concepts has a formal aim:

> I would like to show with precise examples that in analysing discourses themselves, one sees the loosening of the embrace, apparently so tight, of words and things, and the emergence of a group of rules proper to discursive practice. (*The Archaeology of Knowledge*, p. 49)

There is a related set of the effects of an analysis, not all of which can be predicted. But the effects are real. Truth is not a relation indicating a legitimate, or justified, correspondence between word and object. It is not a coherent relationship between words and thoughts. It is the winning set of discursive practices at any given moment. Truth, then, will not always be beauty and justice; but it will always be instructive.

Here is one final concrete example from Foucaultian epistemology, the terms of which are now familiar. The description of the coming to be of psychology relates all the concepts discussed in this section.

> ...it is precisely here that psychology was born—not as the truth of madness, but as a sign that madness was now detached from its truth which was unreason and that it was henceforth nothing but a phenomenon adrift, *insignificant* upon the undefined surface of nature. An enigma without any truth except that which could reduce it.
>
> This is why we must do justice to Freud...Freud went back to madness at the level of *language*, reconstituted one of the essential elements of an experience reduced to silence by positivism; he did not make a major addition to the list of psychological treatments for madness; he restored, in medical thought, the possibility of a dialogue with unreason. (*Madness and Civilization* , p. 198)

Understanding

Foucault is not that far from Spinoza and Plato in linking knowledge and morality. It is extremely doubtful that he would put things in those terms. He would be more likely to say that care for the self is a necessary requirement for participation in the production and analysis of powerful discourses now, and that care for the self requires knowledge and understanding.

Four rules for the direction of thinking come to mind as those Foucault may endorse for his particular practice of epistemology. The first is, quite simply, to read and study everything. In an interview he says:

> One can read all the grammarians, and all the economists. For *The Birth of the Clinic* I read every medical work of importance for methodology of the period 1780-1820. The choices that one could make are inadmissible, and shouldn't exist. One ought to have read everything, study everything. In other words, one must have at one's disposal the general archive of a period at a given moment. And archaeology is, in a strict sense, the science of this archive. (*Foucault Live*, p. 3)

In addition to reading everything, which he assures us we can do if the research is sufficiently focussed, one must make the tools of analysis particular to the period and institution under examination.

> We are faced with the unavoidable fact that the tools that permit the analysis of the will to knowledge must be constructed and defined as we proceed, according to the needs and possibilities that arise from a series of concrete studies. (*language, counter-memory, practice*, p. 201)

There is no foreordained, right set of practices to study. What we study, we must approach not so much naively, but absent the ordering structures which already define the discourse. We must come to a body of knowledge after sliding the conceptual framework away from its disciplinary ordering. This makes up the third rule. Basically, here we are enjoined to ask the right questions. These questions are not the obvious ones. One might imagine that when analyzing the discourses of mental illnesses we should analyze the symptoms of a disruptive set of behaviors. Instead, we should ask who is speaking in a given discourse. Which words are accorded the possibility of making truth? When we think about the doctor we need not concern ourselves only with what is printed and disseminated. We must ask, "what are the institutional sites from which the doctor makes his discourse?" Additionally we must consider the relevant subjects in the discourse, asking what are the various groups informing those subjects. A final rule involves suspending our assumptions about coherence, order and sense. "The history of ideas usually credits the discourse that it analyses with coherence" (*The Archaeology of Knowledge*, 149). We should not make that recurring mistake.

In sum, then, Foucault does not have what might be considered a pure epistemology; still he has one that is not discontinuous with the history of philosophy. The aim of analysis is clarity and understanding in an effort to be a better person and to create a better world. If there is a radical break, in which Foucault does not believe, it is that he does not believe that there is an underlying reality which we must strive to know nor does he believe that there are any formal principles the discovery of which will result in eternal truths.

Criticism

Foucault has been heavily criticized for his views on truth and his views on knowledge. Rather than delineate those by school or individual I have posed them as questions to Foucault.

Who observes the external relations?

It seems specious to argue that there is no interior mental process while at the same time arguing for two levels of externality. How are we to make sense of observation if there is nothing in the individual that is capable of observation? If the levels of outside are as described, it is difficult to imagine how they could ever change. Another way of putting this is if language is prior to discourse but prior to language there is no brute experience, just an always already thinking and doing embedded in these contexts, couldn't we, indeed wouldn't we, end up with radically similar subjects?

Isn't Foucaultian understanding a totalizing one?

Foucault makes vehement arguments against those whose systems intend to explain everything. Such systems inevitably end up prescribing courses of right action, which work themselves out on the bodies of individuals in ways that minimize their freedom. And yet it seems that he sees a major aim as that toward understanding. Isn't he allowing himself what he denies those he criticizes?

Where does freedom fit into power relations?

It appears that Foucault just assumes freedom. His argument that freedom is the case because different individuals respond in different ways in similar contexts does not carry sufficient rigor. The description of discourses at the very best seems to make certain persons disproportionately more free than others with little hope for a reversal of that arrangement. Where does power fit into the tight network of mobile power relations?

Aren't some discourses eternally and universally true?

Some questions seem settled. That is, hasn't science come upon any system of thought that is both eternally and universally true? The theory of gravity has served us well for several centuries. In Philosophy some systems of logic are considered to be indisputable. Aren't there systems of thought which are not discourses?

Why assume power?

Most ontologies posit concrete things at their foundation. Common sense, not always the best philosophical tool, might indicate that at root we have substance. Why make power the sine qua non of existence? Maybe power is illusory and doesn't exist. As a name for complicated relationships in the realm of politics, economics, or personal relationships, it is a useful heuristic for understanding lived reality. There is no reason to suppose that there is such a thing as power.

3

The Politics of Power

Over the course of his career, Foucault has been accused of many things—of mirroring the technologies of power in the discourses he purports to critique (Baudrillard), of misreading Descartes (Derrida), and of being shot through with nihilism, a doctrine stating that all systems of belief are groundless, that values are baseless, and that nothing can be accurately communicated. Foucault's predecessor, who was also accused of nihilism, is Nietzsche. Nietzsche thought it cowardly to fail to face the constructions that are traditionally called eternal human knowledge, despite the grave risks imminent in such an endeavor. Nietzsche guards against the risk of becoming passive in the face of nothing by delineating several positions. One position is that of discipline. Nietzsche argued consistently that only at the end of a disciplined analysis of the genealogy of particular bodies of knowledge is one able to understand that there is only socially constructed knowledge. It is not enough merely to scoff at the order of things; one must know the genesis of that order before one chooses to either reject that order or consciously accept it.

The risk of passivity remains. Even at the end of a disciplined study, one can respond to the results in a cynical manner. This cynical passivity was repugnant to Nietzsche, and he referred to such persons as 'empty nihilists'. Generously showering his scorn upon such sorry cynics, Nietzsche urged them to shrug off their resentments and take the path toward a gay science, using irony as their primary tool of survival and analysis. This is the course Foucault chooses in his epistemology, and also in his politics. And indeed, there is a glee present in Foucault's writing, a Nietzschean glee that his readers find infectious. However, he does not help matters regarding his alleged nihilism when he writes words such as:

> What, do you imagine that I would take so much trouble and so much pleasure in writing, do you think that I would keep so persistently to my task, if I were not preparing—with a rather shaky hand—a labyrinth into which I can venture, in which I can move my discourse, opening up underground passages, forcing it to go far from itself, finding overhangs that reduce and deform its itinerary, in which I can lose myself and appear at last to eyes that I will never have to meet again. I am no doubt not the only one who writes in order to have no face. Do not ask who I am and do not ask me to remain the same. (*The Archaeology of Knowledge*, p. 17)

The above passage illustrates not only Foucault's Nietzschean glee, but also a distinct evasiveness and a fervent desire for freedom from categorization, as if to locate and name him, to give him a face, would be death. Foucault also consistently maintains a close guarding of his work from those who would classify it into positions, views, and similitude, and he has made much of his omission from systematic party politics. This apparent nihilism is tightly linked with a criticism that Foucault holds no positions, politically or otherwise, that he *can not*, both because his method will not allow it, and given the multiplicity and invisibility which is his stated aim.

The criticism that he takes no positions is both true and false. It is true that he is not eager to be pinned down, classified, or transmogrified into a series of lists under the gaze of academics and politicos, and is particularly uninterested in being tied to an architectonic position from which micro-positions might be identified or derived. Such endeavors run the risk of deploying the very technologies of discipline that Foucault has sought to combat. Still, in particular struggles, he is not shy about pronouncing very specific preferences and strategies that he not only espouses but also on which he acts. The following analysis of his politics of power aims to dispel these criticisms against him in addition to examining the outlines of the theory. In so outlining I am trying to leave his methodology as mobile as he intended it while not shying away from tying him to the specific political positions he fervently held.

Power

Deleuze says of Foucault's work that his "general principle is that every form is a compound of relations between forces" (*Foucault*, p. 124). Others have put it more crudely by saying that for Foucault, power is everything. I prefer the Deleuzian description. In what we have observed so far in Foucault's own words, there is a layering of, or a doubling of, interactive arenas. Forces are the foundational layers, if we might allow ourselves to talk this way. Still, forces are the stuff from which discursive and power relations form themselves. For Foucault there is no thing whose description does not include an analysis of power. In some interviews he excepts the physical sciences about which he says little, but usually in the same breath, he directs his interlocutor to the numerous studies linking the development of advances in Chemistry, for example, to economic interests.

By inclination and training, however, he limits himself to what are called the human sciences and here he has found no place, however, tiny, where contradictory powers are not at work. Sometimes when he is writing about something quite unrelated to the analysis of power, a tacit assumption slips in that power is always already present. So for instance when discussing the methods of maintaining order among those classified mentally ill he writes things like: "Unchained animality could be mastered only by *discipline* and brutalizing" (*Madness and Civilization*, p. 75). Whether Foucault is consistent in his descriptions of how he comes to use power as a category of analysis, the analyses of actual political struggles using the category are incisive and ruthlessly political. Let us return to the case of Pierre Riviere, examining it this time under the rubric of coming to terms with political power.

Pierre Riviere is not an exceptional criminal. He slaughters his family, is apprehended, tried in a court of law, found guilty of the murder and then sent to a different prison to await the decision of whether or not he will be executed. But before the pronouncement concerning his sanity can be made, he takes matters in his own hands and kills himself. What is different about Riviere is that he possesses an eerie level of self-consciousness about his crime, both before and after its execution. He had planned to write his confession prior to killing his family, then performed the deed first.

What Foucault seizes on here, what his disciplined analysis reveals to him, is that the France of 1835 saw the legal and medical professions jockeying for status, for the power necessary to assert their discourse as dominant. Riviere's memoir served as the document which could provide the possibility of interpretations that could further the projects of the medical and legal professions. For instance, if it is decided that Riviere performed his crime in full possession of his faculties, he could be pronounced a monster and could be capitally punished. The competing interpretation was that Riviere was insane, and should therefore be institutionalized. The text detailing his crime obtains in a covalence with the crime itself, though these all but disappear among the deployment of power, which asserted itself through the interpretive texts of the medical and legal professionals.

So while in prison, Riviere writes his confession, which he subtitles "Particulars and explanation of the occurrence on June 3 at la Faucterie by Pierre Riviere, author of this deed." Foucault's analysis includes:

> Riviere, there is little doubt, accomplished his crime at the level of a certain discursive practice and of the knowledge bound up with it. In the inextricable unity of his parricide and his text he *really* played the game of the law, the murder and the memoir which at this period governed a whole body of "narratives of crimes." Was it an irrational game? The majority of the jury seem to have decided that the fact that he played this familiar game both in the text and in the deed, that he was the dual author and appeared as the dual subject, was monstrous rather than insane. (*I, Pierre Riviere*, p. 209)

The power relations at work are complex. An interesting feature of Foucault's account is that Riviere is accorded a non-symmetrical but significant amount of power in the set of relations. There is no excusing Riviere's action in Foucault's account, but significantly there is no condemnation. Foucault is stunned at the beauty of Riviere's memoir, and he gives this feature of the text as his reason for its publication. The analysis of the text, however, brings into focus that everyone in the discursive practice has power and is in power. While the ostensible reason Riviere offers for committing his crime is to free his father from his tribulations, he is able to manipulate the popular discourse such that he achieved another purpose: glory in death. There were songs about him, discussions about him, public spectacles surrounding him.

Foucault collects the documents together showing the competing power fields of the law, the medical profession, the popular imagination and Riviere's own sickness and skill:

> In short, his deed/text was subjected to a threefold question of truth: truth of fact, truth of opinion, and truth of science. To a discursive act, a discourse in act, profoundly committed to the rules of popular knowledge there was applied a question derived elsewhere and administered by others. (*I, Pierre Riviere*, p. 210)

Judgment from Foucault on these matters is not forthcoming. However, let us not ignore the possibility that Riviere himself is not outside the application of such questions; that with his aim to achieve glory in death, just as the professionals were attempting to achieve glory in life, Riviere surfaces as this double, the double who is at once erased and whose very prominent feature is his assertion of the 'I', the author. Perhaps Foucault's judgment is not forthcoming because to do so, to make a pronouncement of his own, would necessitate a kind of polarization. To view a person under the label of Monster, or Lunatic, to reduce the systems of power to one monolithic beast, does make it feel easier to deal with. But it does not account for the complicity inherent in our silence, even in our seeming absence from the scene, nor does it admit to the network of discursive practices which have formed this 'monster' (or, for a more recent example, Time magazine's labeling of Yugoslav President Slobodan Milosevich as "The Face of Evil"). For the 'monster' is just the epiphenomenon of such practices. So that is the level which interests Foucault; such a pronouncement would seem beside the point. What is more important for Foucault, as we will see later, is finding a strategy.

We know however from interviews that one of his views on justice is that it is possible to have a popular court of justice, that is, a people's court. The unveiling of the multiple powers at play in the life and death of Pierre Riviere and his family forces the reader to think about justice in a deeper and a more political way. The questions one asks oneself when confronted with these documents cannot be abstract. Questions as "Is capital punishment good or bad?" or "Should psychiatry have power in legal arenas?" reveal themselves to be practically laughable. The questions one must confront are: "What use of power can justice wield that is legitimate?" "What effect does popular discourse about crime have on the subjectivazation of so-called powerless individuals?" "What power do I deploy?" "What accountability do I abnegate?" "To what extent do I encourage criminality by my complicity in the production of the various 'truths'?" and so on. And indeed, such thought is dangerous. Deleuze offers the following reasons for Foucault's thought being dangerous:

> Foucault always evokes the dust or murmur of battle, and he saw thought itself as a sort of war machine. Because once one steps outside what's been thought before, once one ventures outside what's familiar and reassuring, once one has to invent new concepts for unknown lands, then methods and moral systems break down and thinking becomes, as Foucault puts it, a 'perilous act,' a violence whose first victim is oneself. The objections people make, even the questions they pose, always come from safe ashore, and they're like lifebelts flung out, not to help you, but to knock you down and stop you getting anywhere: objections come from lazy, mediocre people, as Foucault knew better than anyone. (*Negotiations*, p. 103)

Bio-Power

Foucault theorized that during the nineteenth century a new form of power comes on the scene. He calls it bio-power. We have been introduced to it as a productive factor in capitalism (Chapter Two). Bio-power is a form of relations that exert themselves not as a means to the death of those in its purview, but as a means of regulating life itself:

> If one can apply the term bio-history as the pressures through which the movements of life and the processes of history interfere with one another, one would have to speak of bio-power to designate what brought life and its mechanisms into the realm of explicit calculations and made knowledge-power an agent of transformation of human life. (*The History of Sexuality*, p. 143)

Sovereign, or monarchical power, in Foucault's view was not as interested in regulating the life of its subjects. It kept its power by being magnificently in control of the ultimate trump card, cessation of life:

> For the first time in history, no doubt, biological existence was reflected in political existence; the fact of living was no longer an inaccessible substrate that only emerged from time to time, amid the randomness of death and its fatality; part of it had passed into knowledge's field of control and power's sphere of

> intervention. Power would no longer be dealing simply with legal subjects over whom the ultimate dominion was death, but with living beings, and the mastery it would be able to exercise over them would have to be applied at the level of life itself; it was the taking charge of life, more than the threat of death, that gave power its access even to the body. (*The History of Sexuality*, p. 142-3)

The immense preoccupation with regulating sexual behavior in this and the last century, Foucault argues, becomes possible because of power's growing presence in individual's lives. A result of this power is that it does not have to take care of the life it regulates and normalizes. Foucault notes that "outside the Western world, famine exists, on a greater scale than ever; and the biological risks confronting the species are perhaps greater, and certainly more serious, than before the birth of microbiology" (*The History of Sexuality*, p. 143). Thus, traditional notions of what power's responsibilities are fall away, and we find there instead the responsibility of power to classify, hierarchize, measure, quantify, appraise, label, etc. It is not only the governing bodies—the state apparatuses—which are implicated in this practice but also courts of law, medical practice, and scientific inquiry. These loci of discursive power have as their aim producing 'normal' people. "A normalizing society is the historical outcome of a technology of power centered on life." (*The History of Sexuality*, p. 144). When we look to some of the positions Foucault does admit to, we will see in them resistance to the normalizing effects of bio-power.

Strategy

In this chapter we have placed emphasis on the case of Pierre Riviere; it is a simple enough case on which Foucault comments, and we have the benefit of the many documents surrounding it which Foucault has compiled. But the determining factor is that it is simple: the parricide is one locatable act carried out by one person. What would be required to carry out Foucault's archeological project for a more recent, more complex situation, one that demands a strategic action?

A recent case calling for strategic action in American society is that involving student uprising over the sale of items produced in sweat-jobs and by child labor in university bookstores. These struggles have received much media attention and should be well known. To adequately analyze this case would require an analysis of numerous institutions in the field of power. We would have to look at a great number of things: the growing relationship between labor and students, the practices and rhetoric of transnational corporations, labor practices in general and in particular. We would have to analyze university structure and interest, address the growing privatization of both public universities and their bookstores. In many ways, a case such as this would be more interesting. But for now, the simplicity of the Pierre Riviere case provides an arena in which we can introduce strategy.

Foucault has said that the reason he chooses the Riviere case among other competing cases is the beauty of Riviere's writing. The reason that the accompanying documentation is reproduced is explained as follows:

> I think the reason we decided to publish these documents was to draw a map, so to speak, of those combats, to reconstruct these confrontations and battles, to rediscover the interaction of those discourses as weapons of attack and defense in the relations of power and knowledge. (*I, Pierre Riviere*, xi)

As we have seen, everything is always already involved in a struggle, a war over the control and access to power and knowledge. Choosing an accompanying strategy must be informed. But what is a strategy? While Foucault is reluctant to tie himself down by making succinct definitions, we might venture that a strategy is a decentering movement, a reordering of discourses surrounding an object of inquiry (such as madness).

One might object that to so reorder is to merely replace one dominant discourse, one mode of producing truth, with another, and what would be the point of that? One could cite Marx as an example of such autonomous reordering of the world in terms of alienation of labor, modes of production, dialectical materialism, class struggle (which Foucault rejects as an essentialized myth), etc. Or Freud's reordering of consciousness in terms of the id, ego, and super ego, the unconscious, sexual desire, envy, etc. However, such discourses claim to explain history or explain consciousness in a way that Foucault's strategizing does not. For Foucault, a strategy must be decentering—it must recognize its own place within the networks of power, seizing on the boundaries which privilege certain modes of truth production, and destabilize them. Foucault's discussion of the Riviere case is one such strategy; his view of the current role of the intellectual, which we will see later, is another.

Because there is no right strategy, in conventional meanings of right or wrong, the strategy must be chosen after a disciplined study of the relevant information. Foucault says of the documents:

> They give us a key to the relations of power, domination, and conflict within which discourses emerge and function, and hence provide material for a potential analysis of discourse (even of scientific discourses) which may be both tactical and political, and therefore strategic. (*I, Pierre Riviere,* p. xii)

Strategy comes at the end of a course of study, not before. It is tempting when thinking about, for instance, criminal justice, to ask the large questions we referred to at the end of the penultimate section. One would like to be able to have justified true beliefs about incarceration, criminality, human nature, and so on. Even at the level of epistemology, however, we have seen that this is not a luxury available to us. And here too, we must look to strategic possibilities. Foucault offers us:

> Rather than seeking the permanence of themes, images, and opinions, through time, rather than retracing the dialectic of their conflicts in order to individualize groups of statements, could one not rather mark out the dispersion of the points of choice, and define, prior to any option, to any thematic preference, a field of strategic possibilities? (*The Archaeology of Knowledge*, p. 37)

Part of coming to a strategy means recognizing that the categories of thought are not thought cleanly, with clear and crisp boundaries. One would like to be able to distinguish between political thought and moral thought and legal thought. But the practice of morality, politics, and law are hopelessly intermingled in our culture, as are popular images of the same (as the Riviere case shows us). Thus, we see this interpenetration:

> All the sheets disseminated in the 19th century are very conformist and moralistic. They draw a careful distinction between the glorious feats of the soldier and the disgusting deeds of the murderer. In a way, they illustrate the Code and convey the political morality underlying it...The ambiguous existence of these sheets undoubtedly masks the processes of a subterranean battle which continued in the aftermath of the

> Revolutionary struggles and the Empire's wars around two rights, perhaps less heterogeneous than they seem at first sight—the right to kill and be killed and the right to speak and narrate. (*I, Pierre Riviere*, pp. 206-7)

The battles over the public ownership of voice and common criminality produce what the tradition often calls "natural" rights: the right to life and the right to speech. For Foucault, these rights are the result of a struggle over the ownership of their meanings.

In a conversation with Gilles Deleuze, Foucault examines the role of the Intellectual, perhaps in order to venture outside, in a performance of the "perilous act" of thinking, the violence whose first victim is oneself:

> Intellectuals are themselves agents of this system of power—the idea of their responsibility for 'consciousness' and discourse forms part of the system. The intellectual's role is no longer to place himself 'somewhat ahead and to the side' in order to express the stifled truth of the collectivity; rather, it is to struggle against the forms of power that transform him into its object and instrument in the sphere of 'knowledge,' 'truth,' 'consciousness,' and 'discourse' (*language, counter-memory, practice*, p. 207-8)

Which leads us to a discussion of resistance.

Resistance

Resistance is different from strategy. It is less conscious of itself as an activity and is less often textual. Though it need not be passive, it is not as active as strategy. A huge resistance to bio-power, according to Foucault, was the creation of the rights we have just discussed. In order for resistance to occur it must be possible. A quick detour through *The Archaeology of Knowledge* shows us the how it is possible for there to be resistance that is basically an external part of the power relations themselves:

> These relations are established between institutions, economic and social processes, behavioral patterns, systems of norms,

> techniques, types of classification, modes of characterization; and these relations are not present in the object; it is that they are deployed when the object is being analyzed...They do not define its internal constitution, but what enables it to appear, to juxtapose itself with other objects, to situate itself in relation to them, to define its difference, its irreducibility, and perhaps even its heterogeneity, in short, to be placed in a field of exteriority. (*The Archaeology of Knowledge*, p. 45)

As a group, or a group of objects, becomes the object of study they undergo transformations. There is no creation of, for example, a soul or of a human right to happiness. Instead, a certain textualizing of a particular group results in its being read through the various systems as possessing this or that quality. As a consequence the group acquires these properties in its behaviors and in its norms. That is an over simplification that may appear more palatable with the following example from *The History of Sexuality*. Foucault describes resistance to bio-power:

> Moreover, against this power that was still new in the nineteenth century, the forces that resisted relied for support on the very thing it invested, that is, on life and man as a living being. Since the last century, the great struggles that have challenged the general system of power were not guided by the belief in a return to former rights...It was life more than the law that became the issue of political struggles, even if the latter were formulated through affirmations concerning rights. The 'right' to life, to one's body, to health, to happiness...and the 'right' to rediscover what one is and all that one can be, this 'right'...was the political response to all these new procedures of power. (*The History of Sexuality*, pp. 144-45)

Resistance, unlike strategy, is necessary to power relations; power must allow some resistance so that it is not seriously embattled. It occurs in spite of studies we may undertake. Sometimes it is said that there are political struggles, the supposed instigators of which do nothing but reinforce the power structures as they exist. Just as a six per cent unemployment rate is necessary for the smooth functioning of capitalism, every power carries within it at least one resistance. And many of these resistances actually end up supporting the power by, for instance, making power appear less brutal than it is, or making power seem overwhelming, omnipresent, and therefore irresistible. So long as those most oppressed by the relations of power believe themselves to have certain inalienable rights, they are not as likely to think seriously about possible strategies for the overthrow of power relations.

Discipline

Foucault argues that with the advent of bio-power, bodies themselves became proper targets for power. Indeed, he argues in *Discipline and Punish: The Birth of the Prison*, that the disciplines surrounding the prisons, the military and the schools have had as one of their aims and effects the creation of docile bodies. "A body is docile that may be subjected, used, transformed and improved" (*Discipline and Punish*, p. 136). Power needs to create docile bodies since it is they who can most easily, quickly, and decidedly be manipulated, shaped into objects prime for the coursing of power, for addition to the network of power relations, taken up into the dominant discourse, and stripped of their ability or interest to create strategies for decentering the modes of truth-production. It works like this:

> Discipline increased the forces of the body (in economic terms of utility) and diminishes these same forces (in political terms of obedience). In short, it dissociates power from the body; on the one hand, it turns it into an 'aptitude', a 'capacity', which it seeks to increase; on the other hand, it reverses the course of the energy, the power that might result from it, and turns it into a relation of strict subjection. (*Discipline and Punish*, p. 138)

There are many ways to create docile bodies. One way is through the intensely rigid regimen of exercise and punishment in the military. Bodies must be created which are at once stronger than the norm, but also immediately willing and capable of following almost any order. The way of making docile bodies most talked about from *Discipline and Punish* is discipline through observation, in particular through Bentham's invention of the Panopticon, an apparatus for the observation of prison inmates.

> ...Bentham laid down the principle that power should be visible and unverifiable. Visible: the inmate will constantly have before his eyes the tall outline of the central tower from which he is spied upon. Unverifiable: the inmate must never

> know whether he is being looked at any one moment; but he must be sure that he may always be so. (*Discipline and Punish*, p. 201)

The result of such a discourse is not only a docile body. It results in the true sense that one is always under observation. The thought that such a control could properly be exerted over human bodies does not arise in a vacuum. It can only arise in a network of discourses, one aim of which is to control the lives of those participating through them. There is no more monolithic discipline than there is monolithic discourse nor strategy nor resistance. Additionally, it would be false in Foucault's view to demonize any individual political leader, for the network of discursive formations, and a receptivity, must already have been in place for this power to surface and deploy. Similarly,

> 'Discipline' may be identified neither with an institution nor with an apparatus; it is a type of power, a modality for its exercise, comprising a whole set of instruments, techniques, procedures, levels of application, targets; it is a 'physics' or an 'anatomy' of power, a technology. And it may be taken over either by 'specialized' institutions (the penitentiaries or 'houses of correction' of the nineteenth century), or by institutions that use it as an essential instrument for a particular end (schools, hospitals), or by pre-existing authorities that find in it a means of reinforcing or reorganizing their internal mechanisms of power (one day we should show how intra-familial relations, essentially in the parents-children cell, have become 'disciplined', absorbing since the classical age external schemata, first educational and military, then medical, psychiatric, psychological, which have made the family the privileged locus of emergence for the disciplinary question of the normal and the abnormal); or by apparatuses that have made discipline their principle of internal functioning (the disciplinarization of the administrative apparatus from the Napoleonic period), or finally by state apparatuses whose major, if not exclusive, function is to assure that the discipline reigns over society as a whole (the police). (*Discipline and Punish*, pp. 215-16)

Reading a passage such as this makes it hard to credit that Foucault is charged with not taking positions. It is difficult to see him as a great sympathizer with, for instance, a police state. Indeed, Foucault states explicitly that the government exercises disciplinary power on its citizens, maintained through the vehicle of the police, in order to produce docile bodies.

Though the example of the Panopticon is rather dramatic, there are more mundane spaces for discipline. Foucault asserts that "people are held in place by simple means, whether housing conditions, mutual observation, several families sharing one kitchen or one bathroom" (*Politics, Philosophy, Culture*, p. 208). Though the specific instrument of the Panopticon is no longer in use, what are the ways that society maintains the thrust of Bentham's invention in other forms, ways that one has one's visibility demanded, and the unverifiable status of that visibility insured? If so, how are we complicit and receptive to such exercises of power? In what discourses are we embedded to create such a possibility?

Foucault's is a radical call, it seems, to assert that one must take a position so strongly that one's thinking—through of concepts is a "perilous act," a violence, whose "first victim is oneself." But perhaps this violence is to the self that is many, the "groupuscle" for which one selects transformative strategies—technologies of the self. For the self is where one must begin, as Foucault constantly reminds us; it is where Foucault himself begins, so that his writing "in order to have no face" is an instance of this double measure, as Pierre Riviere's writing was, an instance of glory and invisibility, an exposure and a masking, an assertion and a destabilization, a measure that results in a monster of sorts, that creature of frightening shape and appearance, that un-disciplined, non-normal self which is not one.

To further dispel the notion that Foucault takes no political position, that he is a nihilist, let's turn to an examination of three positions he takes without qualification.

Positions

Foucault remarks in *language, counter-memory, practice* that "the theory of the subject is at the heart of humanism." Note the clarity of Foucault's political position regarding the theory of the subject:

> It can be attacked in two ways: either by the 'desubjectification' of the will to power (that is, through political struggle in the context of class warfare) or by the

> destruction of the subject as a pseduosovereign (that is, through the attack on 'culture': the suppression of taboos and the limitations and divisions imposed upon the sexes; the setting up of communes; the loosening of inhibitions with regard to drugs; the breaking of all the prohibitions that form and guide the development of a normal individual). (*language, counter-memory, practice*, p. 222)

This is not to say, however, that Foucault does not have an elliptical stance regarding political action. What follows are three examples of how the general development cited above could be etched out in the real, of how Foucault seizes upon local issues as means for the further dismantling of the theory of the subject as pseudosovereign.

As this book is being written there is a war in Yugoslavia. Many Internet lists have devoted their time to the discussion of that crisis. The Philosophy, Hegel, Peirce, Deleuze, and Foucault lists may well have the war as their major topic of discussion for April and May of 1999. It is curious that on the Foucault list the discussion has centered a great deal on Foucault's position concerning the revolution in Iran. He had visited Iran during the change in power between the Shah and the Ayatollah. Foucault's position was to support the revolution against the Shah. Many intellectuals were opposed to the Shah but unable to support Khomeini. Foucault does not take sides here: it is not his struggle. However, he is unqualified in his support for the collective will of a people. He says of his visit: "personally, I thought that the collective will was like God, like the soul, something one would never encounter. I don't know whether you agree with me, but we met, in Tehran and throughout Iran, the collective will of a people. Well, you have to salute it, it doesn't happen everyday" (*Politics, Philosophy, Culture*, p. 215). Foucault notes that accompanying the will to rid Iranian culture of Western influence, there is a chauvinism complete with the inner contradictions the same will entail. His expressed position is that in the working out of the revolution the contradictions will be addressed.

A second position is elaborated more precisely. He argues against all legislation on sexuality except that which involves sexual violence, or rape, and children. His positions there are in flux. He thinks that it might make sense to turn rape into an offense classifiable as violent assault, not as a sex crime, as to so classify it is to privilege the sex organs, separate them from the rest of the body—a separation which in his view has historically been a zone for power to fecundate. Foucault is additionally interested in figuring out the discourse under which one could define sexual consent for children. He makes no hasty judgments about these latter categories, instead choosing to explore possible ramifications of differing legislation, after having informed himself on existing laws and definitions. (For the complete discussion see pages 178-210 in *Politics, Philosophy, Culture*.)

Finally he takes a position with respect to his own power. While he grants interviews to magazines, journals, and newspapers, he will not discuss his own books on the television. His explanation involves the limited availability of network time and the greater need for younger and less famous thinkers to have access to that time.

> But for someone like me, someone who has plenty of opportunities for self-expression, it seems to me indecent to come and talk about my book. So much so that, when I go on television, it is not to substitute for or to duplicate what I have said elsewhere, but to do something that may be useful and to say something that the viewers don't know about. And in saying this, I repeat, I am not criticizing either book programs or the people who take part in them. If they are young, for example, I can understand perfectly well that they should want to fight for their books to be heard: I might very well have done the same myself once. But now I prefer to leave room for them. (*Politics, Philosophy, Culture*, p. 108)

The above examples of Foucault's thoughts on the struggle in Iran, the question of legislation concerning rape victims and children, and his feelings on television appearances are indeed positions and they are carefully thought out. Furthermore, it is important to remember to that the books on madness have resulted in reforms in the treatment of the mentally ill. The books on justice inform work in Critical Legal Theory which have effects on the groups exerting power through legal discourses. Foucault's archaeological method has resulted in a field of scholarship whose purveyors are known as the New Historians, and has helped previously disenfranchised texts and marginalized authors emerge from around the skirts of the void in history and literature departments, and battles have ensued concerning the construction of the canon and what may count as 'worth' studying. And behind each book Foucault's voice resonates, expressing anger at the treatment of people at the hands of power. Notice the ambiguous stance in the following descriptions of punishment within a discourse:

> Let's imagine a justice that functions only according to a code:

> if you steal, your hand is cut off; if you commit adultery, your sex organs are slit; if you murder, your head is cut off. It's a system of arbitrary and obligatory relationships between the acts and the punishment that sanctions the crime in the person of the criminal...But, if justice is concerned with correcting an individual, of gripping the depths of his soul in order to transform him, then everything is different: it's a man who is judging another and the death penalty is absurd. (*Foucault Live*, p. 165)

One might attribute to Foucault anger at the mistreatment of people but even that is problematic. When discussing the situation in Iran, for example, he does not address the special problems women faced. There are no universal political principle. What he offers is a method of resistance and an articulation of strategies.

Criticism

The omnipresence of power

In the chapter on epistemology we encountered this criticism. Any explanatory model that explains everything is justifiably suspect. Questions unique to the strictly political realm build on those we raised in Chapter Two. What exactly is primary power? That is, it is argued that power is a set of complex relations but it does seem as if power were created *ex nihilo*. If power is everywhere there is no person who is completely powerless. How does one account for individuals for whom there is no resistance, no strategy? Is it denied that such individuals exist? (It seems fairly clear that Foucault rejects the notion that one could be completely powerless.)

Rational consensus

An important figure in twentieth century political theory is Jurgen Habermas. He argues that political problems can be solved through rational discourse toward an optimal consensus. An assumption of his discourse is that people are sufficiently similar each to each that disparate communities can, in theory, come to agreement about affairs of state and affairs of war, so, consequently, of peace. The notion of persons coming to understandings of this sort has to be not just false for Foucault but absurd. It is one thing to resist utopian thought, one might argue, but to acquiesce in a perpetual war seems to be too extreme a position.

Can a micro-politics work?

Twentieth century philosophy concerns itself with motivation. Why should anyone join a revolution? Does it make sense to do one's share in the community when most people won't? These questions have been important to political theorists trying to understand why people should be active revolutionaries. When answering these questions, it can often be stressed that if a person believes that the theory under which he or she is operating is a sound one, motivation will be much easier to adopt and maintain. Thus, if one believes that rational persons can and will reach consensus, acting politically makes sense. What is the motivation to act politically if success is partial and illusory? Since power is both ubiquitous and difficult to analyze, one can never be certain that one is acting wisely.

Is Foucault's work counter-revolutionary?

To the extent that one could embrace Foucaultian method and not feel under obligation to act politically, and, to the extent that no political theory about the right ordering of justice exist, wouldn't it be consistent to retire into comfortable complacency? A careful analysis of the moral theory and its attendant theory of subjectivity is helpful to our thinking.

4
The Withering Away of the Subject

Readers of Marx will recognize his echo in the chapter title. Marx and Engels argue that between the categories social and political, the former has foundational status. A revolution capable of achieving permanence and justice would have to be a social revolution. In the social sphere one finds social relations including, importantly, economic relations. It is at the social level where the value in a society is produced and because of the huge concentration of both power and contradiction one finds there, it determines the practices in the political arena. Politics is therefore determined by the social. A political revolution would always be transitory because the powers in the social will reproduce, according to Marx and Engels, the same state structure in its place. A social revolution, which under capitalism means seizing capital and abolishing private property, would have the effect of rendering the state completely unnecessary. Hence the language "the withering away of the state."

Many Foucaultian concepts find their origin in this theory. The notion of continuously reproduced contradictions moving history finds resonance in Foucault. The death of the subject, which concept has received so much notoriety in philosophical and political circles, is not something that a group of thinkers could plan to enact. Instead, the death of the subject will be complete when the concept "subject" is no longer a useful element of discursive practices. For Foucault, then, "man" or the subject appears as a result of conflicting discourses of power and will disappear when it ceases to be useful to any apparatus of power. Marx writes "when the proletariat announces the dissolution of the existing order of things it merely declares the secret of its own existence, for it is the de facto dissolution of this order of things" (*Karl Marx: Early Writings*, p. 142). His language and the theory upholding it find an echo in Foucault:

> The death of man is nothing to get particularly excited about. It's one of the visible forms of a much more general decease, if you like. I don't mean by it the death of god but the death of the subject, of the Subject in capital letters, of the subject as origin and foundation of Knowledge (savoir), of Liberty, of Language and History.
> One can say that all of Western civilization has been subjugated (*assujettie*), and philosophers have only certified the fact by referring all thought and all truth to consciousness, to the Self, to the Subject. In the rumbling that shakes us today, perhaps we have to recognize the birth of a world where the subject is not one but split, not sovereign but dependent, not an absolute origin but a function ceaselessly modified. (*Foucault Live*, p. 61)

This chapter focuses on morality. For several centuries most of our philosophical tradition has posited a unified, rational subject as the locus of moral actions and thoughts. That is, since the late eighteenth century the moral agent has been a focus of moral theorizing. This has caused readers of the tradition since that time to read earlier theories as using the same kind of subject in their work. Thus, Foucault suggests that when we read Aristotle, for example, our twentieth century reading may well be imputing senses of the self that Aristotle could not have thought at that time. Before we are able to discuss Foucault's moral theory, then, it is imperative that we become acquainted with his theory of the subject.

A Subject is Born

In the preface to *The Order of Things*, Foucault poses himself this question under the heading: The problem of the subject:

> Can one speak of science and its history (and therefore of its conditions of existence, its changes, the errors it has perpetrated, the sudden advances that have sent it off on a new course) without reference to the scientist himself—and I am speaking not merely of the concrete individual represented by a proper name, but of his work and the particular form of his thought? (*The Order of Things*, p. xiii)

Foucault's answer is ambiguous, but falls mostly on the affirmative side of the possible responses. Science will eventually be discussed without reference to the scientist—sooner rather than later for Foucault. Because the most true, that is, the most powerful, discourse, it is one he wants to encourage. For several decades science has practiced what is called puzzle research. This means that there will be some need, sometimes top secret, many pieces for which must be developed. Any given scientist may be unaware of the ultimate aim of his or her research. It is hard to say where the subject-scientist is in such endeavors, although one could discourse readily on the scientist-function.

The reasoning that enables him to think of science being done without an individual scientist is summed up as follows near the end of *The Order of Things*. He writes:

> Before the end of the eighteenth century, *man* did not exist—any more than the potency of life, the fecundity of labour, or the historical density of language...Of course, it is possible to object that general grammar, natural history, and the analysis of wealth were all, in a sense, ways of recognizing the existence of man—but there is a distinction to be made. There is no doubt that the natural sciences dealt with man as with a species or a genus: the controversy about the problem of races in the eighteenth century testifies to that. Again, general grammar and economics made use of such notions as need and desire, or memory and imagination. But there was no epistemological consciousness of man as such. (*The Order of Things*, pp. 308-309)

Three themes help us understand his summary remarks. They concern the transition from man as a species or genus to an agent, language as an ordering system, and economics as the study of human life producing wealth.

Human nature and nature had not been juxtaposed to one another in the classical period. Man was one more category of being falling under the general heading nature. As sciences evolved and new ones developed, merely descriptive categories became less and less useful. Thus, Foucault mentions the category of race, a development of the nineteenth century. It was important in the flow of power that humans themselves become classifiable in ways which "relevant" portions of the population could view as scientific. Mere description gave way to classifications that could easily be traced to interested power discourses. The major transition was that of coming to understand classifications not as ways of carving up a pre-existing nature, but to see them as representations of the mind. Thus, when looking at Biology, man was no longer a category, which picked out one of many living objects; it was a category created by, and representative of, autonomous individuals. This set man apart from all other objects in "nature." The word "man" then picks out a different sort of thing than heretofore.

Language had been perceived largely as a system in which words corresponded to objects. Theories of truth, then, sought to understand this system in an effort to find correct correspondences between words and objects. (The original title of *The Order of Things* is *Les Mots et les Choses*—Words and Things. It is only because other books existed, notably W.V.O Quine's *Word and Object*, bearing strikingly similar titles that its translation is quite different from its first name.) As man became an organizer of things and not merely part of that order, the manners in which linguists theorized language was radically altered. The genesis of words was theorized more as a creative set of actions than as a strict ordering of things under stable concepts.

Finally, economics changed along with these other systems of thought. As the production of value came to be seen as increasingly the result of creative human labor and the fruits of that labor became increasingly tied to the person performing that labor, the sense of economics as the science of knowing one's place diminished. In classical times, the study of economics produced outlines of the correct delineation of subject positions toward a harmonious and organic social function. Men and women, property owners and slaves, each were assigned a separate set of virtues and functions. When each person was seen as producing value him or herself, and not simply receiving the share accorded to each on the basis of social position, economics could not longer assign universal groups of virtues to any given kind of person.

Man is a social construct, then, which functions importantly during a time when diverse ideologies had to be unified into a doctrine of the Same. Every person was said to be every other's moral equal. The qualities assigned every rational being were on the order of capacity for rational thought, freedom, and finally rights. Foucault argues that we are in a time period where power discourses are diverting from this doctrine of the Same. If the trend continues, which he thinks it will do, then the necessity of man will have been exhausted.

Perhaps a concrete example of how a subject comes on the scene will clarify these themes. In *The Birth of the Clinic*, Foucault describes how a particular individual, qua individual, could become the object of discourse:

> The gaze is no longer reductive; it is, rather, that which establishes the individual in his irreducible quality. And thus it becomes possible to organize a rational language around it. The *object* of discourse may equally well be a *subject*, without the figures of objectivity being in any way altered. It is this *formal* reorganization, *in depth*, rather than the abandonment of theories and old systems, that made *clinical experience* possible; it lifted the old Aristotelian prohibition: one could at last hold a scientifically structured discourse about an individual. (*The Birth of the Clinic*, p. xiv)

As the doctors observed the patient they saw the patient as distinct from every other patient. Trends could be observed, to be sure, but the medical gaze was not intended to reaffirm the individual as this sort of object. In other words, it was permissible to look closely at the individual as an object (under the old discourses) but also as a subject with unique desires, phobias, wishes, and problems.

So the individual steps out as an object of theory cognizant that the theorist is likewise an individual. With such a recent birth, many wonder why Foucault is so quick to announce its death.

A Subject Dies

Arrangements of knowledge become increasingly, for Foucault, systems of thought that privilege identity formation for the self. When we looked at confession in the chapter on politics, it was clear that one of the contemporary functions of confession is to stabilize and pinpoint an identity for the speaker that disciplines him or her into a conceptual straight jacket. He argues that one should adopt strategies that hasten the end of stable identities for subjects because the externally defined identities that one finds in dominant power discourses limit the possibilities for positive change. Of course, one cannot will oneself out of prevailing arrangements of knowledge. Concerted effort is required which can only come as a result of a matrix of power relations shifting toward some end. The last words of *The Order of Things* read:

> If those arrangements were to disappear as they appeared, if some event of which we can at the moment do not more than sense the possibility—without knowing either what its form will be or what it promises—were to cause them to crumble, as the ground of Classical thought did, at the end of the eighteenth century, then one can certainly wager that man would be erased, like a face drawn in sand at the edge of the sea. (*The Order of Things*, p. 387)

The method for opening up thought is to examine existing research under the aegis of "man" and to do away with the particular ordering categories that cling to the fiction of "man." His method "uses the results already obtained to define a method of analysis purged of all anthropologism" (*The Archaeology of Knowledge*, p. 16).

Marx is not absent from Foucault's writing on the genesis and demise of the subject; he is missed only as a particularly named subjectivity. Marx saw a subject emerging who could be cognizant of itself as the purging of overlaid alienation. The alienation was "discovered" by Marx through Hegel. What Marx called alienation, Hegel called human nature. Thus putting will into property for Hegel constituted the first step of being human. Marx saw labor of this kind, if appropriated, alienated labor. Hegel saw the freedom to own property as a symbol that humanity had progressed mightily toward freedom. Marx saw this freedom as inequitably distributed, under capitalism necessarily so, and called the social arrangements that facilitated it exploitation. Marx sees emancipation as persons coming to know themselves as the producers of value and acting to own the value themselves. Foucault finds that emancipation is impossible but that moving to a better arrangement means, in part, coming to recognize the contingency of current arrangements of knowledge. In "On the Jewish Question," Marx writes:

> *All* emancipation is *reduction* of the human world and of relationships to *man himself*.
> Political emancipation is the reduction of man on the one hand to the member of civil society, the *egoistic, independent* individual, and on the other to the *citizen*, the moral person.
> Only when real, individual man resumes the abstract citizen into himself and as an individual man has become a *species-being* in his empirical life, his individual work and his individual relationships, only when man has recognized and organized his *forces propres* as *social forces* so that social force is no longer separated from him in the form of *political* force, only then will human emancipation be completed. (*Early Writings*, p. 234)

The moral force in social movements stands outside of the discourse of Marxist revolution. In Foucault, the category of the moral is likewise in transition. One thing should be clear about Foucault's moral theory. It will be always be embedded in a historically specific context: there will be no universal prescriptions in his texts. The moral and the political will be interwoven. Finally, the moral agent will not look much like moral agents who precede it.

Morality

When Foucault is discussing his work in less formal venues, such as a symposium, or an interview, his sense of moral outrage over injustice becomes evident. The moral outrage is almost always coupled with a political situation which must either be resisted or serve as an opening to strategic positioning against or with it. In one such interview, Foucault is discussing a scientist's attempt to perform experiments in the asylum. "He [Basgalia] posed this question: could the victims of the asylum initiate a political struggle against the social structure that denounces them as mad? These experiments were savagely prohibited" (*language, counter-memory, practice*, p. 230). His use of the political and social here shows a departure from Marx that is nevertheless completely dependent on him. That the discussion is political is revealed a little later in the interview. He says: "In more general terms, this also means that we can't defeat the system through isolated actions; we must engage in it on all fronts—the university, the prisons, and the domain of psychiatry—one after another since our forces are not strong enough for a simultaneous attack" (*language, counter-memory, practice*, p. 230). Accustomed as we are to locating moral agency and political possibilities in a stable subject, how can we make sense of his talk here? What subject understands the convergence of institutions resulting in the prohibition of research which would enable persons to better their situations? Why would resisting the stable, unified subject be beneficial in the construction of political strategies?

In the second volume of *The History of Sexuality*, Foucault discusses distinctly moral terms such as "art of existence" and "techniques of the self." No set of rules, nor even a system of analyzing moral propositions, is forthcoming. Still, one comes away from the text with a sense that a moral person is one who learns how to understand oneself with respect to oneself. Furthermore, one senses that one has some sort of obligation to understand the histories of those portions of subjectivity that most inform one. (Two persons reading *The Use of Pleasure* will turn out to focus on different histories or on similar histories for different reasons.) Foucault states explicitly the sort of moral history he is not interested in performing. He explains:

> This does not mean that I proposed to write a history of the successive conceptions of desire, of concupiscence, or of libido, but rather to analyze the practices by which individuals were led to focus their attention on themselves, to decipher, recognize, and acknowledge themselves as subjects of desire, bringing into play between themselves and themselves a certain relationship that allows them to discover, in desire, the truth of their being, be it natural or fallen. (*The Use of Pleasure*, p. 5)

Additionally, "the object was to learn to what extent the effort to think one's own history can free thought from what it silently thinks, and so enable it to think differently" (*The Use of Pleasure*, p. 9). In other words, the genealogy of morals Foucault is exercising over the use of pleasure has as its aim the possibility of transformation through understanding. That the study has an auxiliary aim the understanding of the construction of sexuality as it informs our contemporary self-understanding seems topsy-turvy. The content of a particular study turns out not to be as important to Foucault as what we discover about ourselves in the process of, in his case the writing, and in our case the reading, of the study.

He finds it necessary to explain that he is not interested in the history of concepts in themselves because there are no such universals. One's history, which necessarily includes those conceptual histories that inform one, must be thought and re-thought. This results in an articulation of what had been inarticulate and mute. Once thought consciously, there is a possible space to think about one's relationship to oneself in a different way. As in his other books, each attempt at understanding comes down to finding a better approximation to truth. Foucault concludes that his work resulted in a better perspective on his relationship with himself: "The journey rejuvenates things, and ages the relationship with oneself. I seem to have gained a better perspective on the way I worked—gropingly, and by means of different or successive fragments—on this project, whose goal is a history of truth" (*The Use of Pleasure*, p. 11).

The study confines itself to the first two centuries of Western philosophy and practice surrounding the use of pleasure. The four relationships on which Foucault focuses are with oneself, one's wife, boys, and truth. (Clearly the nascent subject will be male.) The not yet born subject under discussion, and construction, undergoes more transformation in the realm of practice than of theory. Foucault finds that rules of conduct turn out to be much less important than practices of self do. These result in an aesthetics of existence he finds traces of in contemporary morals (and constructions of sexuality). The morality changes over the course of two centuries in clearly identifiable ways. It is interesting that the transformation would not stand out so clearly, had the study confined itself to the study of prescribed, canonical codes of behavior.

Foucault's working definition of morality comes from ordinary language. That is, he does not want his readers to be at a distance from the major concepts of the text. "By 'morality,' one means a set of values and rules of action that are recommended to individuals through the intermediary of various prescriptive agencies such as the family (in one of its roles), educational institutions, churches, and so forth" (*The Use of Pleasure*, p. 25). Morality is not monolithic; the interplay of agencies and individuals creates "a complex interplay of elements that counterbalance and correct one another, and cancel each other out on certain points" (*The Use of Pleasure*, p. 25). One of his findings is that: "there is no specific moral action that does not refer to a unified moral conduct; no moral conduct that does not call for the forming of oneself as an ethical subject; and no forming of the ethical subject without 'modes of subjectivation' and an 'ascetics' or 'practices of the self' that support them" (*The Use of Pleasure*, p. 28). Thinking morally, tantamount to acting morally, is itself concrete practice.

What can we say about Foucault's moral theory from our discussions about subjectivity and morality? First, that one should strive to understand oneself in as many relations as one can. Second, moral rules are not as important as moral practice and understanding our relations will probably proceed more productively if we focus on practice. Finally, that if we start our moral reasoning with universal qualities that we attribute to universal man, we will stray far afield from the practice which should interest us. These modes of thinking can be brought under a rubric of "arts of existence," or "technique of self." Arts of existence are defined as "those intentional and voluntary actions by which men not only set themselves rules of conduct, but also seek to transform themselves, to change themselves in their singular being, and to make their life into an *oeuvre* that carries certain aesthetic values and meets certain stylistic criteria" (*The Use of Pleasure*, pp. 10-11). The specifics of any of these choices are left open—even to Foucault. Throughout the work under discussion, he requests of the reader that he or she attribute to him nothing as confining as a universal prescription.

The Use of Pleasure is also about the construction of sexuality. Foucault argues in the last volume of his history, but also in some earlier essays, that our era is also restrictive about sexuality. In an essay called "Preface to Transgression," he argues that far from being less restrictive about sexuality, our age sets many more limits on the expression of sexuality than he found in studying the early days of the Christian church, for example. At that time, he notes, sexual ecstasy was seen as a limit experience bringing one closer "to the heart of the Divine love." Sexuality functions for us as a determinant of truth of our identity and as such leaves little possibility for the kind of intensity previously experienced and recounted. The immediacy of being which one might encounter in transgressing to a limit experience is completely absent from "the demonic character, who, true to his nature, 'denies everything'." (*language, counter-memory, practice*, p. 37). Foucault can see his way to a possible new way of thinking about sexuality, following in the footsteps of thinkers such as Georges Bataille, but only if he remembers his Nietzsche and does not take the path as some mythic return to an earlier, more noble age. (This is an implicit and significant criticism of Heidegger that may only be noted in passing.)

> In reintroducing the experience of the divine at the center of thought, philosophy has been well aware since Nietzsche (or it should undoubtedly know by now) that it questions an origin without positivity and an opening indifferent to the patience of the negative. (*language, counter-memory, practice*, p. 37)

The divine center is a place where excess can be accessed and made to speak. The silence of, for instance, irrationality can never be total. When it is opened out into discourse there is nothing that can rein it back with the checks of rational discourse. It is not something that can be tamed. The "moral" "subject" will try to understand the excess and bring it to light and speech.

An important relationship between the constructions of sexuality and morality is that when sexuality became a constant repetitive practice of dominant discourses, the death of god, in Nietzsche's sense, followed quickly.

> In this sense, the appearance of sexuality as a fundamental problem marks the transformation of a philosophy of man as worker to a philosophy based on a being who speaks; and insofar as philosophy has traditionally maintained a secondary role to knowledge and work, it must be admitted, not as a sign of crisis but of essential structure, that is now secondary to language. (*language, counter-memory, practice*, p. 50)

It is not that contemporary rules are less rigid; on the contrary transgression is harder to obtain. The practices becomes more rigid as transgression loses it power. An art of existence, a moral practice, might be finding the spaces where transgression still gives way to self-revelatory intensity.

This manner of talking about Foucault's morality reveals itself already as a strategy. There is not one strain of his work here that is given a higher status than any other strategy. One must discuss the construction of sexuality, it seems, because he devotes three volumes to its study in terms of the development of moral and ethical concepts. Furthermore, he argues that the construction of sexuality is sufficiently important that it has fairly direct implications for such things as war and genocide. The discussion through transgression, however, is one of many an interpreter of Foucault could suggest.

Nietzsche also concerned himself with constructions of subjectivity and argued that a new man was on the horizon: the superman. Deleuze delineates Foucault's relationship to Nietzsche in this regard:

> As Foucault would say, the superman is much less than the disappearance of living men, and much more than a change of concept: it is the advent of a new form that is neither God nor man and which, it is hoped, will not prove worse than its two previous forms. (*Foucault*, p. 132)

Language, our contemporary house of being, opens into divine excess. The moral subject will enter that house with hope and understanding and become something different, something potentially better.

Author-Function

One of Foucault's more controversial claims is that the author has died into an author-function. This particular subjectivity is one that is occurring because of changes in the discourse, but also one that authors should actively seek. As such, it provides a concrete example of space where death of subjectivity collides with a moral practice. Foucault discusses writing without a writer to outline two functions of its contemporary deployment. The first quality of writing he notes in the essay "What is an Author?" is that it has freed itself of the need to self-expression. The writing "implies an action that is always testing the limits of its regularity, transgressing and reversing an order that it accepts and manipulates" (*language, counter-memory, practice*, p. 116). The second quality is that writing exhibits a kinship between itself and death. Far from an older tradition whose function was to achieve immortality for the writer and the text's heroes, today's writing underscores the necessary emptying out of the author into the text and out of himself or herself. "Writing is now linked to sacrifice and to the sacrifice of life itself; it is a voluntary obliteration of the self that does not require representation in books because it takes place in the everyday existence of the writer" (*language, counter-memory, practice*, p. 117).

Foucault does not invent these qualities; instead, he reads them off of the lives of writers and draws them from contemporary philosophy of literature and literary criticism. His aim is to understand how to read texts in their most true light. He is also concerned with understanding how to make sense of the author-function that has seemingly replaced the writer. The absence of self-expression is supplanted by a more unified function: "the function of an author is to characterize the existence, circulation and operation of certain discourses within a society" (*language, counter-memory, practice*, p. 124). We must not try to determine the true identity of the writer behind the author because, as he states, it "would be as false to seek the author in relation to the actual writer as to the fictional narrator; the 'author-function' arises out of their scission—in the division and distance of the two" (*language, counter-memory, practice*, p. 129). The contemporary reader looks for connections between texts and the discourses from which they arise instead of discovering the true meaning of the text as it might relate to its author. As he puts it:

> Perhaps the time has come to study not only the expressive value and formal transformations of discourse, but its mode of existence: the modifications and variations, within any culture, of modes of circulation, valorization, attribution, and appropriation. Partially at the expense of themes and concepts that an author places in his work, the 'author-function' could also reveal the manner in which discourse is articulated on the basis of social relationships. (*language, counter-memory, practice*, p. 137)

The reading of the construction of sexuality in the proceeding section could then be seen as Foucaultian itself. The concept "sexuality" becomes less important than the place of the text in discourses surrounding morality and subjectivity. The private aims of Foucault are only discussed when he calls attention to them as instantiations of cultural understandings of coming to know oneself in an age when subjectivity is something other than the vestigial discourses suggest. The whole process is a moral practice that Foucault would endorse, and whose endorsement makes sense only in the context of his alliance and rejection of Marx and Nietzsche.

The Role of the Intellectual

Another form of subjectivity that carries moral import is the intellectual. When Foucault was studying in France Jean Paul Sartre argued forcefully and influentially on the moral and political duty of the intellectual to be engaged. The term "engaged intellectual" indicated a thinker who allied himself or herself with practices consonant with the intellectual labor being undertaken. The academic climate was such that one had to position oneself with respect to this concept of the role of the intellectual. The discussion was one that properly fits under the rubric of the moral.

Foucault was irritated at the privileging of personalities. Consistent with his method, a struggle is always understandable and important in terms of the contested power relations and not this or that person. He thought that texts should be able to circulate as thought thinking itself and that their merits alone would determine their strategic power in the realm of discursive power. The discussions about the death of the author and the engaged intellectual continue, however, during times when the academic star was in conceptual rising. An author who was in popular favor could immediately dominate a discussion when a better, less famous, interpretation existed. Foucault suggests:

> There is a solution, however: the only law on the press, the only law on books, that I would like to see brought in, would be a prohibition to use an author's name twice, together with a right to anonymity and to pseudonyms so that each book might be read for itself. There are books for which knowledge of the author is a key to its intelligibility. But apart from a few great authors, this knowledge, in the case of most of the others, serves absolutely no purpose. It acts only as a barrier. For someone like me—I am not a great author, but only someone who writes books—it would be better if my books were read for themselves, with whatever faults and qualities they may have. (*Politics, Culture, Philosophy*, p. 53)

Foucault gives a more positive description of the role of the intellectual in an interview on power and sex. He is asked if he is able to augment Marx's work in a way which will hasten the revolution. Refusing that question on the grounds that intellectuals are no longer prophets he offers the following picture of what he thinks an intellectual should look like.

> I dream of the intellectual who destroys evidence and generalities...who, wherever he moves, contributes to posing the question of knowing whether the revolution is worth the trouble, and what kind, it being understood that the question can be answered only by those who are willing to risk their lives to bring it about...it is the question of today. (*Politics, Philosophy, Culture*, p. 124)

The intellectual and the author-function are not separate entities. An intellectual who is sufficiently mobile to be in a potion to be asked such risky questions knows better than to speak for a group. Once a group is named the group is thereby identifiable and hence a target. Significantly, the place where the moral force and practice of the two concretely moral subjectivities come together is neither in a static text, nor in an interview where one person is attempting to get to know the views of the other more important person—the writer. In a conversation, later titled "Intellectuals and Power" Foucault and Deleuze come to agreement about the relationship of intellectuals to power. Deleuze speaks for both of them when he comments:

> A theorizing intellectual, for us, is no longer a subject, a representing or representative consciousness. Those who act and struggle are no longer represented, either by a group or a union that appropriates the right to stand as their conscience. Who speaks and acts? It is always a multiplicity, even within the person who speaks and acts. All of us are "groupuscules." Representation no longer exists; there's only action-theoretical and practical action, which serve as relays and form networks. (*language, counter-memory, practice*, pp. 206-207)

On any given subject, for instance, prisons, the speech, the writing, which ultimately matters in asking the question of the day, is that of the group opposed to power. Foucault says: "And when the prisoners began to speak, they possessed an individual theory of prisons, the penal system, and justice. It is this form of discourse which ultimately matters, a discourse against power, the counter-discourse of prisoners and those we call delinquents—and not a theory *about* delinquency" (*language, counter-memory, practice*, p. 209).

Opening up discourse to the groups of discussion does not always yield the picture of humanity we are accustomed to seeing. One notes in the study of morality, that the emphasis on a single, unified moral agent as the primary locus of action leads to strange interpretations in fields outside of morality. Thus, a popular interpretation of World War II involves a Hitler who operates as a solitary devil. There is no historical account that would lead a rational person to hold such a view, but it is a common and widespread belief rarely challenged. It is the sort of silent discourse one allows oneself against all evidence. Deleuze exposes the dangers of thinking and discoursing in this manner. "But of course we never desire against our interests, because interest always follows and finds itself where desire has placed it. We cannot shut out the scream of the Reich: the masses were not deceived; at a particular time, they actually wanted a fascist regime!" (*language, counter-memory, practice*, p. 215). If we only oppose power that shows itself in historical individuals, we risk repeating history's worst offenses, as current events show too well.

Criticism

Criticism of Foucault in the moral realm is not as widespread as it is in the political and epistemological arenas. This is due, in part, to the difficulty of reconstructing the moral theory. The slippage of categories is nowhere more noticeable than between the moral and political. I have suggested in my reconstruction that the slippage is inevitably because Foucault has already taken up certain of Marx's categories where the slippage is already apparent. The political theory receives more comment because many of Foucault's readers find the political concerns more pressing—and with good reason. Nevertheless, criticism does exist to which we now turn.

It's a Boy

Foucault largely ignored feminism and even, in important ways, women. Many feminists have nevertheless appropriated some of his methodological and conceptual frameworks in positive ways. Sometimes this is done grudgingly because the subject who is born and who is in the process of disappearing is identifiably male and only male. This in itself is justification for criticism. Feminist works were available to Foucault, and in many cases his consulting it would have improved his work. For instance, parallel to his development of the theory of docile bodies, feminists were working on the constructed bodies of women. The methodological tools available to him were ignored.

Some more specific feminist criticisms of Foucault's moral theory include erasure of agency, feminist identity, and theories of sexuality. With respect to agency, some feminists had argued since Simone de Beauvoir introduced the concept in the Fifties that one was not born a woman but becomes a woman. This specific coming to subjectivity, also coming out of, but not wed to, a Marxist framework, detailed extensively a genealogy of morals which calls into question Foucault's interpretation of changes occurring in the late eighteenth century. Beauvoir argues that the Subject is male and at the margins of history is a female consciousness who must adopt certain male characteristics to be recognized as a Subject in her own right. This double history, ignored by Foucault, would necessitate changes in his account of the coming to subjectivity of the autonomous individual.

Feminist interpretations of identity are as varied as are the feminists who produce them. It is fair to say, however, that for many feminists personal identity is an important step in the consciousness raising required to be a political actor. That is, if one's culture denies one the status of agent—legally, morally, politically, domestically—then an important first step in resisting power or strategizing against it involves recognizing oneself as autonomous. An upshot of Foucault's moral theory is that one should resist such subjectivication. For men, it could be argued, this is an easy abnegation. For women in certain circumstances it is tantamount to suicide.

Finally many feminists had produced painstaking accounts of the construction of sexuality based on a gender, sex distinction worked out in the fields of psychoanalysis, economics, sociology, linguistics, and many other fields. There were already accounts of the construction of sexuality in philosophy such that men could only come to consciousness, and hence to their sexuality, by being recognized by women. Foucault completely ignores this body of work to the detriment of his theory.

Agency and Freedom

The qualities that have traditionally defined the moral agent: autonomy, rationality, freedom, consistency, and so on are not posited in Foucault's account. It could be argued that the absence of any of these traits results in an account of some practice, but it cannot be a moral practice. If the agent is not even an agent, then how can one be said to act morally or immorally? An example of criticism from one branch of moral theorizing stands as illustrative of the way other criticisms would go.

Deontology is the study of morality which holds that one should perform an action simply because the action is right. One must eschew consequences as a guide to moral reasoning and actions because when one considers consequences, one throws one's motivation into instrumentality. The most noted deontologist is probably Immanuel Kant. His argument against lying is elegant and persuasive to many people. Basically he argues that a good will is the only good in itself and it is striving for a good will that rational persons do. A good will is good to the extent that its motives are pure. When a rational person considers telling an untruth a contradiction occurs in his or her willing. Telling a lie contradicts human nature, which knows intuitively that truth is good because it is logically consistent. (This gloss is too abbreviated to capture Kant's reasoning but the interested reader may read the argument in *Groundwork for the Metaphysics of Morals*.)

The force of criticism from other moral theories is that most moral theories that have remained in currency appeal to intuitions many of us can embrace. Few of us think that it permissible to lie, for example. Kant offers compelling arguments that substantiate our intuitions as imminently rational. A criticism from outside, such as this one, asks of the supporter of Foucault, how does your theory account for the obvious wrong in lying? Persons making this criticism do not think that Foucault's answer that morality is a practice determined by context is acceptable. The risk appears too great.

The Genesis of Desire

For many philosophers desire is a foundational category. That is, they believe that there is something like true desire that can function as the impetus to knowledge or survival or the instantiation of self-interest. Judith Butler articulates the manner in which desire is constructed for Foucault. It is part of a complicated criticism of Foucault's possible lapse into dialectics that I will not treat here. Her exposition of the construction of desire through discourse makes the theory clear. She writes:

> For Foucault, desire is the inadvertent consequence of the law. And insofar as the law is reproduced through given discursive practices, these latter participate in the cultural production of desire. In a political elaboration of structuralist premises, Foucault argues that (a) language is always structured in a specific historical form and is, therefore, always a kind of *discourse*, and (b) that this discourse invariably recapitulates and produces given historical relations of power, and (c) these

> power-laden discourses produce desire through their regulatory practices. (*Subjects of Desire*, p. 218)

Desire is a third order category that does not originate in the subject, in the individual. It is produced external to the subject at the level of discourse. The three views alluded to above find this construction of desire untenable. For thinkers as diverse as Spinoza and Plato, desire for knowledge is the impetus behind all moral practice. If desire is created by discourse then morality is thrown into a relativity that is absolutely repellent to a Platonist and moderately so to a Spinozist. Those who see desire as the primary reason that humans stay in existence also would find themselves in a position to reject Foucault. The construction of desire as Foucault sees it would render inexplicable their foundational assumption that persons desire to persist in existence. Finally, philosophers who view self-interest as a foundational category would have to dismiss Foucault's moral theory for the position that desire is constructed. Theories of the construction of sexualities or ontologies of the same might find reason to question Foucault on this matter.

5
Care of the Self

Choosing how to read a thinker's work, or outlining the direction it takes, is always an act of will. For me, Foucault's work culminates in a concept he calls "Care of the Self." Indeed, Foucault, while putting his own work in context, justifies this reading. In summarizing the journey he took, he explains:

> Let's say very briefly that through studying madness and psychiatry, crime and punishment, I have tried to show how we have indirectly constituted ourselves through the exclusion of others: criminals, mad people, and so on. And now my present work deals with the question: How did we directly constitute our identity through some ethical techniques of the self which developed through antiquity down to now? (*Technologies of the Self*, p. 146)

In other words, the self for which one will be asked to care is one that is variously constituted. On the one hand, we are constituted through the exclusion of others from the categories we wish to claim as defining "us." We are sane because others are insane. We find ourselves good against a measure of others as "delinquent." Our identities are formed, additionally, through the appropriation, consciously and unconsciously, of the ethical systems that have "won," or been most powerful, throughout the ages. One could suggest that an unconscious determinant does not make much sense when it involves ethical principles and practices. How can we be determined by the ethics of early Christian monks or by ancient and obscure philosophers if we don't know anything about them? For Foucault, these discourses permeate our contemporary discourses—their traces are everywhere to be found in the working out of power. To know ourselves, to care sufficiently for ourselves, unraveling these power networks is necessary. To engage in an aesthetics of existence, we have to remember that we exist external to the constructed notions of "soul," "mind," and "self. Thus the question "What are we today?" forces us into an arena that is, for Foucault, "historical reflection on ourselves" (*Technologies of the Self*, p. 145). There have been changes that allow us a greater freedom in the analysis of ourselves. Foucault suggests that it is to our advantage that we need not renounce ourselves in order to think seriously in the ethical realm. For instance, Marx and Freud move us past individuality and transparency with respect to self-knowledge. Indeed, contemporary discourse encourages us to invent ourselves and this, for Foucault, is a positive change. The practices required to care for ourselves are many, especially since for Foucault, caring for ourselves requires caring for others. The main concepts involved in self-care are: will to knowledge, sexuality, confession, and recognition of our external constitution.

Will to Knowledge

Care of the self is tied up with deciphering the social relations that culminate in the construction of truth. These are not based in Foucault's intuitions about ethics or the self but are the result of his research presented in volumes one through three of the *History of Sexuality*. For Freud, the civilization had to come to terms with its death instinct in order to avert widespread or total destruction, due to unacknowledged aggression. For Foucault such acknowledgment requires understanding far more than the constitution of the human subject as a bundle of instincts warring within themselves. Instead the obligation becomes noticing how the discourse that results in talking about humans as things with an unconscious and deep inner life becomes formed in the first place. He writes, "the care of the self—or the attention one devotes to the care that others should take of themselves—appears then as an intensification of social relations" (*The Care of the Self*, p. 53).

> Social relations are to be understood only at the end of a historical analysis of their formations. Doing ethics then

> becomes a rather monumental effort. In addition to examining the playing out of this intensification of social relations, the person striving to care for himself or herself will have to remember that the journey involves an analysis of truth. "The task of testing oneself, examining oneself, monitoring oneself in a series of clearly defined exercises, makes the question of truth—the truth concerning what one is, what one does, and what one is capable of doing—central to the formation of the ethical subject" (*The Care of the Self*, p. 68).

That this was Foucault's aim throughout his studies is evident in many passages. I choose here to cite from disparate chronological periods in an effort to show that the moral and political concerns were present alongside the epistemological concerns. Their coexistence stems from Foucault's careful attention to both teaching and self-transformation—concepts with which we began this essay on his work. In *Madness and Civilization*, he is already working the ways in which a new moral subjectivity comes into being while the mad are being classified as our other. In order to sort out our ethical principles, this exclusion must be noted. He writes:

> What had been blindness would become unconsciousness, what had been error would become fault, and everything in madness that designated the paradoxical manifestation of non-being would become the natural punishment of a moral evil. In short, that whole vertical hierarchy which constituted the structure of classical madness, from the cycle of material causes to the transcendence of delirium, would now collapse and spread over the surface of a domain which psychology and morality would soon occupy together and contest with each other. (*Madness and Civilization*, p. 158)

A later example occurs in the last years of his life. He argues that the nature of the self we have constituted through our collective understandings of rationality makes it impossible for the unexamined self to act at once politically and effectively. "I should say that in everyday political rationality the failure of political theories is probably due neither to politics nor to theories but to the type of rationality in which they are rooted" (*Technologies of the Self*, p. 161).

What are we today? What is the self for which we are supposed to care? For those who wish to control us, we are souls, docile bodies, or constructions of subjection made more malleable by discipline. The antidote to these self-perceptions is to notice that they are external constructions. Foucault urges us to remember, or come to know, that

> What counts in the things said by men is not so much what they may have thought or the extent to which these things represent their thoughts, as that which systematizes them from the outset, thus making them thereafter endlessly accessible to new discourses and open to the task of transforming them. (*The Birth of the Clinic*, p. xix)

The intensification of social relations is what we are capable of doing once we shrug off classifications which limit our possibilities for thinking, and hence, for acting. Care for self is a kind of teaching—to oneself and to others that results in transformation. One cannot forget history properly, that is, one can not be rid of historical social relations which inhibit rather than enhance pleasure and experience, until one knows the history to forget.

Studying history must itself be a transformation. Foucault is interested in the increasing disappearance of codes; interestingly, this disappearance does not seem to be accompanied by a lessened sense of guilt nor by a heightened sense of pleasure. Losing prohibition, in itself, is insufficient for transformation. What can take the place of moral codes in a world where there cannot be reasonable justification for such codes? How can the study of histories of specific moral codes help us find an ethic that is mobile? Foucault notes that "if I was interested in Antiquity it was because, for a whole series of reasons, the idea of a morality as obedience to a code of rules is now disappearing, has already disappeared. And to this absence of morality corresponds, must correspond, the search for an aesthetics of existence" (*Politics, Philosophy, Culture*, p. 49). An aesthetics of existence is the right sort of thing to fill the void left by the disappearance of moral codes. Foucault does not want to set up a new code; he is not even interested in prescribing liberation or tolerance. (They have their downfalls and hidden discourses!) Recognizing the need for some direction, his excursions through history are partial attempts to find possible replacements for the codes which do not require renouncing the self, which do not prohibit, and which are ruthlessly clear that selves are accountable for themselves and others. This aesthetics could serve as exemplary without falling into subjectivizing discourse. He sums up the duty in this regard, leaving the lion's share of care of the self to individuals:

> People have to build their own ethics, taking as a part of departure the historical analysis, sociological analysis and so on, one can provide for them. I have to provide ethical principles or practical advice at the same moment, in the same book and the same analysis. All this prescriptive network has to be elaborated and transformed by people themselves. (*Politics, Philosophy, Culture*, p. 16)

Not returning to traditional philosophical discourse—we have seen that he does not believe in the return—he finds that position of opposition and convergence with respect to philosophy, which optimizes a joyous care for the self.

> I would say at this point that philosophy is a way of reflecting on our relation to the truth. But it must not end there. It's a way of asking oneself: if such is the relation that we have with truth, then how should we conduct ourselves? I think that it has done and continues today to do a very considerable and multiple labor, which modifies at the same time both our connection to the truth and our way of conducting ourselves. And this in a complex conjunction between a whole series of researches and a whole set of social movements. It's the very life of philosophy. (*Foucault Live*, p. 201)

The will to knowledge, then, is in the power field as a discourse and in the power field as a kind of force. The will, which humans have more or less of depending on the current positioning of discourses, is severely limited by the constructions of sexuality under which we find ourselves. One of the discourses that dominate our contemporary world is, for Foucault, that of sexuality. Sexuality is seen by many to be the most significant determiner of our identities. Indeed, psychoanalytic theory, before its being taken up by feminist theorists, had coming to consciousness as necessarily tied up with the coming to a particular kind of sex specific identity.

Sexuality

The will to knowledge is tied up with constructions of sexuality. Sexuality has become an increasingly discoursed topic. Foucault thinks that it is interesting that sexuality is both a truth-producing discourse and that the proliferation of truth and prohibition surrounding sexual practice and moral codes increases sexual misery. He offers suggestions for overcoming this misery. Foucault may very well resist this last point because it tends to an over-generalization about care of self. What works for one person may be devastating for another. The point is that the individual has the power to overcome the conditioning of the power discourses if the art of existence is essayed. Foucault reminds us again that "it is not power, but the subject, which is the general theme of my research" (*Michel Foucault: Beyond Structuralism and Hermeneutics*, p. 208-209). With this introduction we will examine these three stages of sexuality as they relate to care for the self.

Foucault raises an interesting and important question:

> How is it that in a society like ours, sexuality is not simply a means of reproducing the species, the family, and the individual? Not simply a means to obtain pleasure and enjoyment? How has sexuality come to be considered the privileged place where our deepest "truth" is read and expressed? (*Politics, Philosophy, Culture*, p. 110-111)

He recognizes that there is a partial explanation for the epistemological importance given to sexuality because it is a means of dividing up which kind of persons are allowed access to the truth. Foucault never makes the move to a feminist critique of the epistemology of the categories of sexuality. The critique is latent however. It is in keeping with his reticence to speak for others which may have kept him from making the critique explicit.

Importantly, too, in the absence of misery about sex, this connection of truth with sexuality allows "free men" a sense of the freedom that the discourse required for some people. (See *The Use of Pleasure*, p. 253.) It is also interesting that in producing the categories of sex a science of sex was produced which inhibited pleasures as it increased and proliferated, but designed a pleasure of its own:

> Perhaps this production of truth, intimidated though it was by the scientific model, multiplied, intensified, and even created its own intrinsic pleasures. It is often said that we have been incapable of imagining any new pleasures. We have at least invented a different kind of pleasure: pleasure in the truth of pleasure, the pleasure of knowing that truth, of discovering and exposing it, the fascination of seeing it and telling it, of captivating and capturing others by it, of confiding in secret, of luring it out in the open—the specific pleasure of the true

> discourse on pleasure. (*History of Sexuality, Volume One*, p. 71).

The pleasure of talking about sex, obsessing about it, all the while pretending that we are not talking about it, but prohibiting it, takes a nasty turn when the prohibitions make a loud discourse producing subjectivities that make freedom in sex difficult. Foucault discusses such prohibitions on homosexuality in interviews. He is also concerned with the creation of children's sexuality which resulted in observances and practices which denied the sexuality that the discourse itself had created:

> A specific "sexuality of children" was constituted—precautions, dangerous, constantly in need of supervision. This resulted in a sexual misery of childhood and adolescence from which our own generations still have not recovered (*Politics, Philosophy, Culture*, p. 113).

Foucault is not the sort of philosopher who will describe an overcoming of this misery in general or universal terms. His discussions concerning the practices of sado-masochism are instructive nevertheless. There is an attention to the detail of retaining some prohibition but within an arena of freedom. He says:

> What interests the practitioners of S & M is that the relationship is at the same time regulated and open. It resembles a chess game in the sense that one can win and the other lose. The master can lose in the S & M game if he finds he is unable to respond to the needs and trials of his victim. Conversely, the servant can lose if he fails to meet or can't stand meeting the challenge thrown at him by the master. This mixture of rules and openness has the effect of intensifying sexual relations by introducing a perpetual novelty, a perpetual tension and a perpetual uncertainty which the simple consummation of the act lacks. The idea is also to make use of every part of the body as a sexual instrument. (*Foucault Live*, p. 226)

So there is an overcoming which can occur if one recognizes the constructed nature of that relationship, but also if one is able to recognize that the external tensions are the loci of experience. That recognition of the unavailability of the internal experience is paramount to coming to understand oneself. It is also crucial that there is a noticing of the created internal as an important place for silence, friendship and the creation of meaning.

Recognition of our external constitution

Caring for oneself involves intensifying experience, as we just saw. Intensifying experience, in turn, requires noticing that experience is constructed outside of ourselves. There is not a pre-given interior attempting to work itself out into power relations. The subject is thrown into the set of power relations available to it. It has the freedom to choose from amongst the positions it might adopt. Additionally it has the possibility of creating an ethics, which is not a self-renunciation of a contingently constructed self. Sexual ethics is an example that works well in Foucault's thinking:

To understand how one can find pleasure without the intense self-awareness our culture tells us exists, it is helpful to return to the epistemological description of Foucault's project. This time our focus will be on the relation between the possibility of thinking and feeling pleasure, for our immediate purposes here, without an actual interior self. Deleuze as always is helpful:

> Up until now, we have encountered three dimensions: the relations which have been formed or formalized along certain strata (Knowledge); the relations between forces to be found at the level of the diagram (Power); and the relation with the outside, that absolute relation, as Blanchot says, which is also a non-relation (Thought). Does this mean that there is no inside? Foucault continually submits interiority to a radical critique. But is there *an inside that lies deeper than any internal world*, just as the outside is farther away than any external world? The outside is not a fixed limit but a moving matter animated by peristaltic movements, folds and foldings that together make up an inside: they are not something other than the outside, but precisely the inside of the outside. *The Order of Things* developed this theme: if thought comes from outside, and remains attached to the outside, how come the outside does not flood into the inside, as the element that thought does not and cannot think of? The unthought is therefore not external to thought but lies at its very heart, as

> that impossibility of thinking which doubles or hollows out the outside. (*Foucault*, pp. 96-97)

Foucault is interested in this void, this silence, this nothingness. If we are to experience fully this life and its multiple pleasures, we "must make the intelligible appear against a backdrop of emptiness, and deny its necessity. We must think that what exists is far from filling all possible spaces. To make a truly unavoidable challenge of the question: what can we make work, what new game can we invent?" (*Foucault Live*, 209). Foucault has been saying that we have to be careful in how we describe and act homosexuality so that it doesn't turn into law and prohibition. This turn to the epistemology of articulation is crucial. Modern society chatters ceaselessly, turning us away from the possibility of silence and while over-valuing the secret. If we recognize our place as signified as well as signifiers, we will not waste our energies battling the paper tiger of prohibition. (Foucault has been criticized for positing this kind of power in everyone. He recognizes that some people's prohibitions are flimsier than others; he is ruthless in his "assumption" that individuals are accountable.)

That the theorist who brings us the "confession" as the marker of an age gone mad with self-revelation of the "wrong" self, would call for an ethos of silence is telling. Foucault writes: "silence was then a specific form of experiencing a relationship with others. This is something that I believe is really worthwhile cultivating. I'm in favor of developing silence as a cultural ethos" (*Politics, Philosophy, Culture*, p. 4). The confession comes into full flowering around the construction of sexuality. Rejecting the confession is a good place to reclaim the pleasure prohibition steals.

Confession

> Let there be no misunderstanding: I do not claim that sex has not been prohibited or barred or masked or misapprehended since the classical age; nor do I even assert that it has suffered these things any less from that period on than before. I do not maintain that the prohibition of sex is a ruse; but it is a ruse to make prohibition into the basic and constitutive element from which one would be able to write the history of what has been said concerning sex starting from the modern epoch. (*History of Sexuality, Volume One*, p. 12)

Against this appealing pull to silence is the endless chit-chat of people revealing their secrets. The prohibitions on sex make an entry into its discipline, which focus attention on *scientia sexualis* at the expense of an *ars erotica*. But,

> On the face of it at least, our civilization possesses no *ars erotica*. In return, it is undoubtedly the only civilization to practice a *scientia sexualis*; or rather, the only civilization to have developed over the centuries procedures for telling the truth of sex which are geared to a form of knowledge-power strictly opposed to the art of initiations and the masterful secret: I have in mind the confession. (*History of Sexuality*, p. 58)

Foucault suggests that our culture's version of telling the truth about sex runs in counter-distinction to the *ars erotica*, which in Greece functioned more as a practioner's guide to sex; it was a pedagogical tool designed to transmit a knowledge for the production of the pleasure and enjoyment of sex, whereas the truth-telling practice surrounding sex in our civilization, which boomed in the seventeenth century in the form of authorized discursive formations—the confession—served to expose the secret of the subject.

Such discourse, however, under the auspices of institutions (the church, the bourgeois family) proliferated in Foucault's view under a rather specific set of conditions: it became comprised of lists of deviant behaviors (in distinction to 'normal' sexual practices—see chapter three on normalization, strategy and resistance), measures of the degree of intensity the discourse obtains in the subject, classifications of the psychoanalyzed subject into labels of hysteria, repression, etc., appraisals of the subject in the church confessional which obtain amid censorship, denials, and defenses; hierarchizations of the body into zones of sexual acceptability, neutrality, or the tabooed, etc. This *scientia sexualis*, this ordering of sex's knowledge, allowed discourses concerning sex to multiply and fecundate, even if this meant that they were to take shape among the mosaic of the secret, the taboo, the censored, the prohibited, the exotic, the illegitimate, the pathological.

Such groupings and orderings are but the epiphenomena of the discourse of power-knowledge which has, Foucault suggests, coursed through our sense of sexuality—even the existence of the notion of sexuality itself—more sharply since the seventeenth century. In *The History of Sexuality*, Foucault's stated aim is to examine

> the case of a society which has been loudly castigating itself for more than a century, which speaks verbosely of its own silence, takes great pains to relate in detail the things it does not say, denounces the powers it exercises, and promises to liberate itself from the very laws that have made it function. (*The History of Sexuality* p. 8)

Foucault rejects what he terms "The Repressive Hypothesis," doubting that sexual repression, which so many of us have accepted as a distinct marker of our age, is a historically established fact at all. Foucault asserts that, far from being 'repressed,' our culture's history of discourses on sex are not marked by a break whereby we remain silent about sex in our repression, but are talking about sex more than ever, albeit about the Secret of sex, the Hidden sex, the Mysterious sex, the Prohibited, Censored sex, the sex Which Dare Not Speak its Name, etc. They are all, however disingenuous, discourses concerning sex. This rift marks the moment for Foucault's entry into an archaeological analysis concerning the play of power-knowledge through sexuality, sexuality's discursive practices and their roles in the production of truth, as well as the technologies which have been power's modes of deployment. Among these technologies is the confession, to which we now turn our attention.

Foucault contends that a mastery over sex was needed as the evolution of Catholic confession manuals demanded "discretion" in the descriptions of the sexual act, though the scope of such confessions continually increased. This mastery would find its hold in language:

> The Christian Pastoral prescribed as a fundamental duty the task of passing everything having to do with sex through the endless mill of speech. The forbidding of certain words, the decency of expressions, all the censorings of vocabulary, might well have been only secondary devices compared to the great subjegation: ways of rendering it morally acceptable and technically useful. (*The History of Sexuality*, p. 21)

However, it is not only the confessional proper which exercised this double action in the discourses surrounding sex; it became disseminated throughout the culture as Foucault describes below:

> With the rise of Protestantism, the Counter Reformation,

> eighteenth-century pedagogy, and nineteenth-century medicine, it gradually lost its ritualistic and exclusive localization; it spread; it has been employed in a whole series of relationships: children and parents, students and educators, patients and psychiatrists, delinquents and experts. The motivations and effects it is expected to produce have varied, as have the forms it has taken: interrogations, consultations, autobiographical narratives, letters; they have been recorded, transcribed, assembled into dossiers, published, and commented on. (*The History of Sexuality*, p. 63)

Foucault insists, however, that it is not merely the description of the sex act which is demanded of the confessing subject—it is the circumstances surrounding the act which one must provide: the confessor is expected to produce an assessment of the obsessions, images, quantity of pleasures, frequency, deviations, etc.

It is worth noting at this point the continuation of certain foci between Foucault's work on confession in the context of sexuality, and in the case of Pierre Riviere discussed in Chapter Three. Riviere, who wrote a confession of his own for the courts in 1835, and had it perused by the large stable of legal and medical professionals, (as well as intellectuals on the late twentieth-century scene), had his first "confession" rejected. During Riviere's early interrogations, he insisted that he performed his crime after he was visited by an angel of god, who told him that god wanted Riviere to kill his family. When prosecutors dug deeper, and Riviere dismissed the story of the angel, they were finally satisfied with an explanation for the murders whereby Riviere committed his crime in a rage after his mother left his father's bed. This demonstrates for us not only the continuity of Foucault's writing, but the manifold shapes which confession can take, and the emphasis on a disclosure of sex in a confession, however far afield the subject may seem.

Let us also note that Pierre Riviere was caught between multiple moments of confession: the confession of his crime both before it was committed and after—the imagining of a confession, and, importantly, the contextualization of his act as that which obtains qua confession, the writing and reconstruction (which calls into question exactly what is being reconstructed—the crime or the imagined confession), as well as the subsequent modes of interpretation which sought the truth of his act in the rhetoric which at once performed a disclosure and an occulting. The will to knowledge is the sinecure for confession. Where confession reveals nothing of interest in the care for the self, willing knowledge about the external self reveals possibilities for an artful existence.

Foucault is a teacher, who like many of his teachers, wanted nomadic students and no disciples. There are reasons not to be his disciple. The assumption of power as omnipresent is problematic. Many will be unable to accept a notion of desire as always constructed. Whatever the ultimate truth of the theory of discourse, some would argue that even if it is the "absolute" truth, one should dissemble at the level of politics because the problem of motivation is so significant in the twentieth century. Whatever the philosophical reasons, there is the compelling human reason. He gives us so much and asked of his readers only that we read him as part of series of competing discourses. There should be no Foucaultians—only Foucaultian concepts and Foucaultian methods.

Bibliography

Burchell, Graham, Colin Gordon and Peter Miller, Eds. **The Foucault Effect: Studies in Governmentality, with Two Lectures and an Interview with Michel Foucault**. Chicago: University of Chicago Press, 1991.

Butler, Judith P. **Subjects of Desire: Hegelian Reflections in Twentieth Century France**. New York: Columbia University Press, 1987.

Deleuze, Gilles. **Foucault**. Trans., Ed. Sean Hand. Minneapolis: University of Minnesota Press, 1988.

-----. **Negotiations**. Trans. Martin Joughin. New York: Columbia University Press, 1995.

Deleuze, Gilles and Claire Parnet. **Dialogues**. Trans. by Hugh Tomlison and Barbara Habberjam. New York: Columbia University Press, 1977.

Foucault, Michel. Preface. **Anti-Oedipus: Capitalism and Schizophrenia**. By Gilles Deleuze and Felix Guattari. Trans. Robert Hurley, Mark Seem, and Helen R. Lane. Minneapolis: University of Minnesota Press, 1983.

-----. **The Archaeology of Knowledge**. Trans. A.M. Sheridan Smith. New York: Pantheon Books, 1972.

-----. **The Birth of the Clinic: An Archaeology of Medical Perception**. Trans. A.M. Sheridan Smith. New York: Vintage, 1994.

-----. **The Care of the Self: The History of Sexuality, Volume Three**. Trans. Robert Hurley. New York: Pantheon Books, 1986.

-----. **Death and the Labyrinth: The World of Raymond Roussel**. Trans. Charles Ruas. Berkeley: University of California Press, 1987.

-----. **Discipline and Punish: The Birth of the Prison**. Trans. Alan Sheridan. New York: Vintage Books, 1995.

-----. **Foucault Live**. Trans. John Johnston. Ed. Sylvere Letringer. New York: Semiotext(e), 1989.

-----. **Introduction. Herculine Barbin: Being the Recently Discovered Memoirs of a Nineteenth-Century French Hermaphrodite**. Trans. Richard McDougall. New York: Pantheon Books, 1980.

-----. **The History of Sexuality Volume I: An Introduction**. Trans. Robert Hurley. New York: Vintage Books, 1980.

-----. **I, Pierre Riviere, having slaughtered my mother, my sister, and my brother: A Case of Parricide in the 19th Century**. Ed. Foucault. Trans. Frank Jellinek. Lincoln: University of Nebraska Press, 1975.

-----. **language, counter-memory, practice: selected essays and interviews by Michel Foucault**. Ed. Donald F. Bouchard. Trans. Donald Bouchard and Sherry Simon. Ithaca: Cornell University Press, 1977.

-----. **Madness and Civilization: A History of Insanity in the Age of Reason**. Trans. Richard Howard. New York: Vintage, 1988.

-----. Hubert L. Dreyfus and Paul Rabinow, Eds. **Michel Foucault: Beyond Structuralism and Hermeneutics**. Second Ed. Chicago: University of Chicago Press, 1983.

-----. "Maurice Blanchot: The Thought from Outside." **Foucault/Blanchot**. Trans. Jeffrey Mehlman and Brian Massumi. New York: Zone Books, 1987.

-----. **The Order of Things: An Archaeology of the Human Sciences.** New York: Vintage, 1973.

-----. **Politics, Philosophy, Culture: Interviews and Other Writings 1977-1984**. Ed. Lawrence D. Kritzman. Trans. Alan Sheridan and Others. New York: Routledge, 1988.

-----. **Power/Knowledge: Selected Interviews and Other Writings 1972-1977**. Ed. Colin Gordon. Trans. Colin Gordon, Leo Marshall, John Mepham, Kate Soper. New York: Pantheon Books, 1988.

-----. "The Political Technology of Individuals." **Technologies of the Self: A Seminar with Michel Foucault**. Ed. Luther H. Martin, Huck Gutman, Patrick H. Hutton. Amherst: University of Massachusetts Press, 1988.

-----. **This is not a pipe**. Trans. and Ed. James Harkness. Berkeley: University of California Press, 1983.

-----. **The Use of Pleasure: The History of Sexuality, Volume Two**. Trans. Robert Hurley. New York: Vintage Books, 1990.

Hegel, G.W.F. **Phenomenology of Spirit**. Trans. A.V. Miller. Oxford: Oxford University Press, 1977.

Kant, Immanuel. **Groundwork for the Metaphysics of Morals**. Trans. James W. Ellington. Indianapolis: Hackett, 1981.

Marx, Karl. "A Contribution to the Critique of Hegel's Philosophy of Right." **Early Writings**. Trans. Gregor Benton. Ed. Quintin Hoare. New York: Vintage, 1975.

-----. "A Critique of Hegel's Doctrine of State." **Early Writings**. Trans. Rodney Livingstone. Ed. Quintin Hoare. New York: Vintage, 1975.